LAPIDARY

FOR PLEASURE & PROFIT

Mexican coconut.

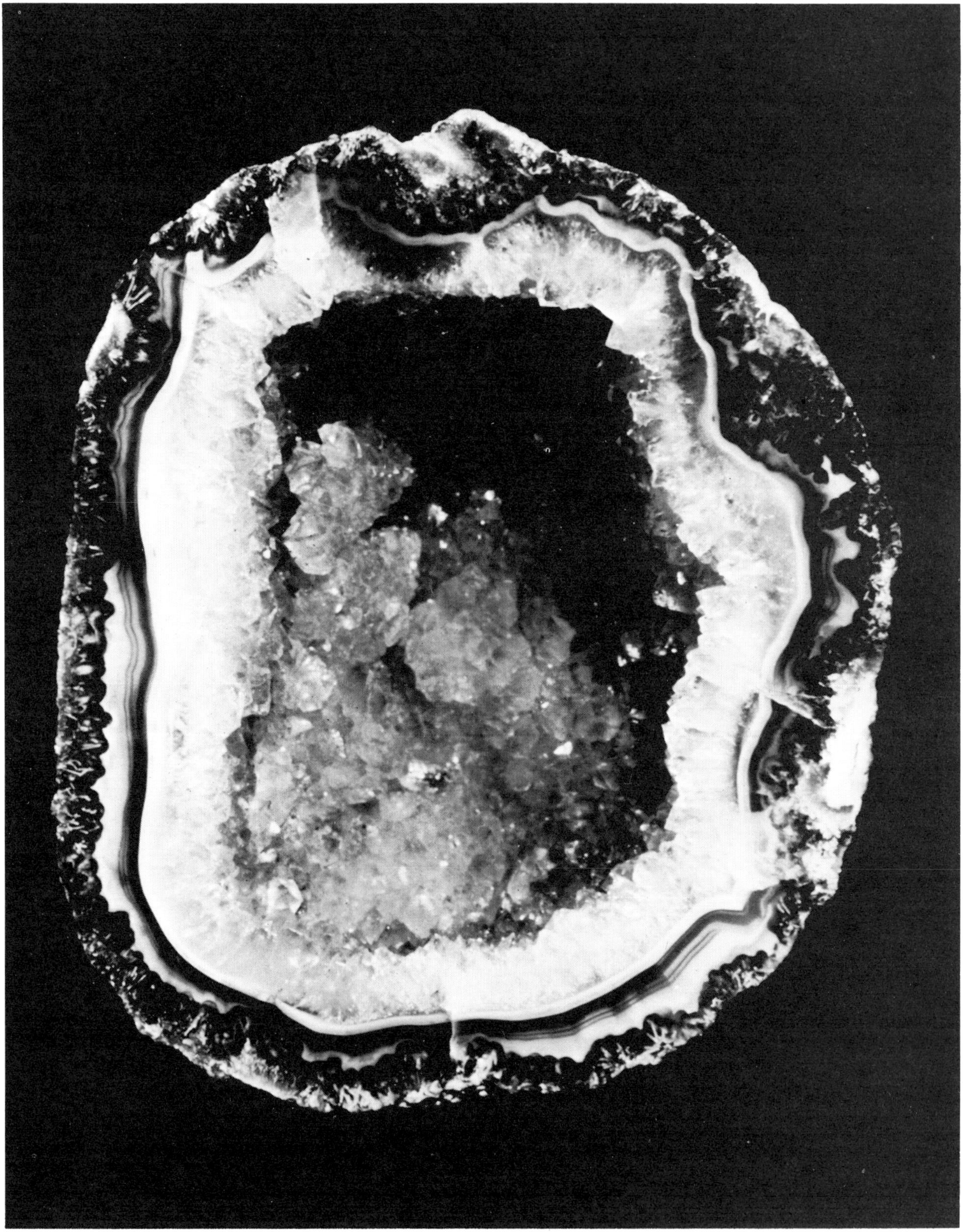

ERIC SHORE

LAPIDARY FOR PLEASURE & PROFIT

JOHN GIFFORD
LONDON

ISBN 0 7071 0591 9

First published 1978 by
John Gifford Ltd
125 Charing Cross Road
London WC2H 0EB

Line drawings by Leslie C. Benenson

Designed by Melvyn Gill Design Associates

Printed in Great Britain by Biddles Ltd, Guildford, Surrey

CONTENTS

INTRODUCTION 6

CHAPTER ONE
Gemstones 7

CHAPTER TWO
Sawing 10

CHAPTER THREE
Grinding 21

CHAPTER FOUR
Sanding 33

CHAPTER FIVE
Polishing 41

CHAPTER SIX
Combination Machines 48

CHAPTER SEVEN
Lapping 56

CHAPTER EIGHT
Cutting a Cabochon 65

CHAPTER NINE
Tumbling 77

CHAPTER TEN
The More Common Gemstones and their Treatment 85

APPENDICES 94

LIST OF SUPPLIERS 95

INTRODUCTION

I have written this book to pass on the experience and enjoyment gained through practicing the art of lapidary for the past seven years. Quite deliberately I have refrained from producing working drawings of the machines built for school use or those made for myself at home. The ideal machine for one person will not suit the next.

I wish to thank my family for the understanding shown when I have not been available to them while writing this book. My thanks also to my headmaster, Mr. R. A. F. Springate, for allowing me to introduce a new craft into his school, and to Mr. T. C. Burnard, Wiltshire Craft Organiser, for his help and encouragement over the years. I am also indebted to my colleagues and past students for the help which they gladly gave to build some of the machinery shown in this book.

I thank the many firms for their offers of help and Wiltshire County Council for allowing me to photograph the school equipment; also the following firms for supplying photographs for my use: Ammonite Ltd., Avon Gems, M. L. Beach, Gemstones Ltd., Hirsh Jacobson Merchandising Co. Ltd., The Gem Rock & Lapidary Centre, Wessex Gems & Crafts, Whithear Lapidary Co.

Eric Shore

1. GEMSTONES

Until recently the art of lapidary was undertaken by very few, but with the arrival of new techniques and materials, it has become a very popular hobby. The word *lapidary* is derived from the Latin *lapis*, meaning stone, hence lapidary—a person who cuts and polishes stone.

The material used by the amateur lapidary is very varied, ranging from the expensive stone bought from a dealer to the ordinary pebble from the beach. Amber, jet, coral, ivory and various shells are also used, and although these cannot be classed as stone they are usually included in modern books on gemmology.

Precious and semi-precious are terms used to differentiate between expensive and not so expensive stones; but where is the line drawn between the two? The more modern usage of the word 'Gemstone' tends to cover all materials that can be cut and polished.

The qualities of gemstones

What are the qualities we need to look for to distinguish gemstone from ordinary rocks and minerals? The most important must be beauty, for without it no rock or mineral can give pleasure to the beholder. The vivid colours of rubies, sapphires and emeralds are attractive to the eye, as are the bandings on an agate or the apparent movement of lines of colour on a tiger-eye.

Most gemstones are made into jewellery and they must stand up to being rubbed, dropped and knocked against hard objects. Durability, therefore must be considered. The stronger, harder stones will continue to sparkle and gleam for very much longer than their metal settings. Many stones are quite soft yet are still cut and polished because of their great beauty. Probably the best example of this type of stone is the opal. As a general rule though, most gemstones are tough and hard.

Rarity must also be considered as it is the main factor governing price. This is not really a quality of a gemstone but more an attitude of mind. Many synthetic gems can be made as beautiful as natural gems, yet most people will choose the latter because of their higher value, although in many instances even a trained eye cannot spot any difference.

There is little doubt that beauty is the main quality of a gemstone. Rarity can be governed to some extent by man—holding back supplies to keep the price up—and durability can be overcome by cementing clear quartz on to a softer stone, as will be shown later.

Gemstone rough

Rough material can be split into two main groups:

(a) Clear crystal material used mainly for faceted gems. This is a way of shaping stones by cutting tiny flat surfaces, called facets, on the top and bottom of the stone. Particular patterns and angles are used to make the gem sparkle more than would otherwise be possible.

(b) Opaque stones, which would not be improved by faceting, as insufficient light would pass through. These are cut in a dome shape called a cabochon, as are some clear crystals with mineral inclusions.

Rough material for cabochons is usually sold by the pound, with rarer material sometimes sold by the ounce, gram or even carat; good quality faceting grade is sold by the gram or carat. To give some idea of size, a gram is 5 carats and a piece of quartz about the size of a small pea weighs roughly 5 carats.

As more and more dealers are opening, rough material can be bought in several ways. All dealers will send rough by post and a few will send rock on approval, though the big disadvantage of buying this way is the cost of postage on heavy material. The best way is to visit your nearest dealer and select your own material.

Rough can also be bought ready cut into slabs, which are usually between 3/16 in and 3/8 in thick, and is sold by the square inch. This is probably the most expensive way of buying, but if you do not possess a slabbing saw it will save many hours of work. The other advantage of buying slabbed material is that most flaws and waste will have been eliminated.

The other way to obtain rough, which gives the greatest pleasure, is to find your own and successfully cut and polish it.

Moh's scale of hardness

Hardness is defined as resistance to scratching, and must not be confused with toughness. Moh's scale of hardness is used by the lapidary to denote the degree of hardness of any gemstone. On this scale the hardest mineral known, diamond, is given the value of 10, and the softest, talc, the value of 1.

Talc	1
Gypsum	2
Calcite	3
Fluorite	4
Apatite	5
Feldspar	6
Quartz	7
Topaz	8
Corundum	9
Diamond	10

At first this scale can be confusing, as it may give the impression that diamond is only twice as hard as apatite: in reality it is many times harder. All of these minerals will scratch one with a lower value but not those with a higher value.

2. SAWING

As with most raw materials, a piece of rough rock is of little use to the lapidary until it has been broken down into usable sizes. The easiest and most convenient way of doing this is to use a diamond saw. Basically, this is similar to a woodworker's circular saw, with a blade mounted on an arbor, the main difference being a tank, mounted beneath the table, holding a liquid coolant for the blade to run in.

Blades vary in diameter and thickness from 0.010 × 4in to 0.075 × 24in and bigger. The smaller thinner blades, sometimes called 'slitting' saws, are normally used for valuable stones where the waste needs to be kept to a minimum. Up to 10in saws are termed 'trim saws', and larger than this are called 'slabbing saws'. The trim saw with an 8 to 10in blade is probably the best for the amateur lapidary, as most of the cutting he is likely to attempt can be done on such a machine. The amount of slabbing that can be done on a 6in trim saw is very limited, and a 12 or 14in slabbing saw is very expensive to buy.

Saw blades

The first time a diamond saw is seen in action, the observer is usually amazed to see how apparently negligent the operator is in allowing his fingers to move so close to the revolving blade. His astonishment is complete when the operator demonstrates

Plate 1 McBurnley Rock Rascal 6in trim saw.

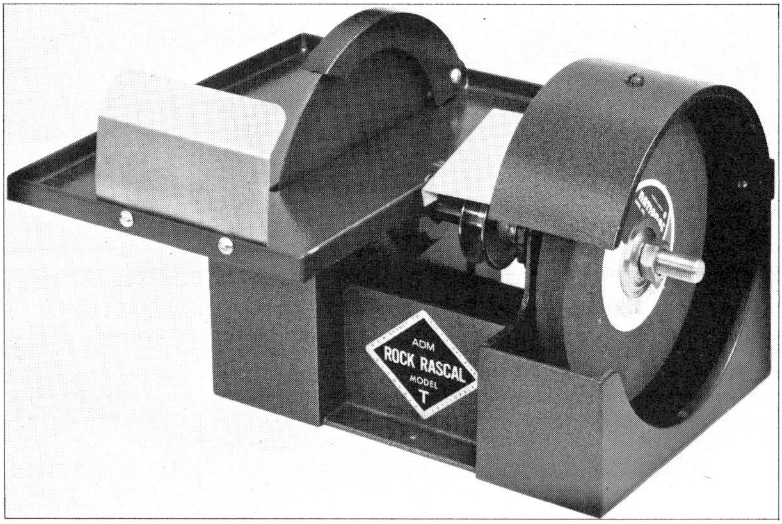

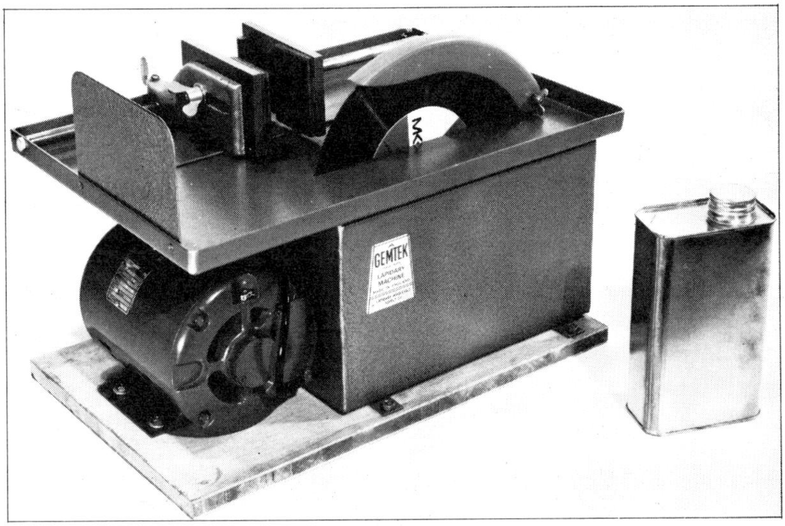

Plate 2   The Gemtek 10in trim saw.

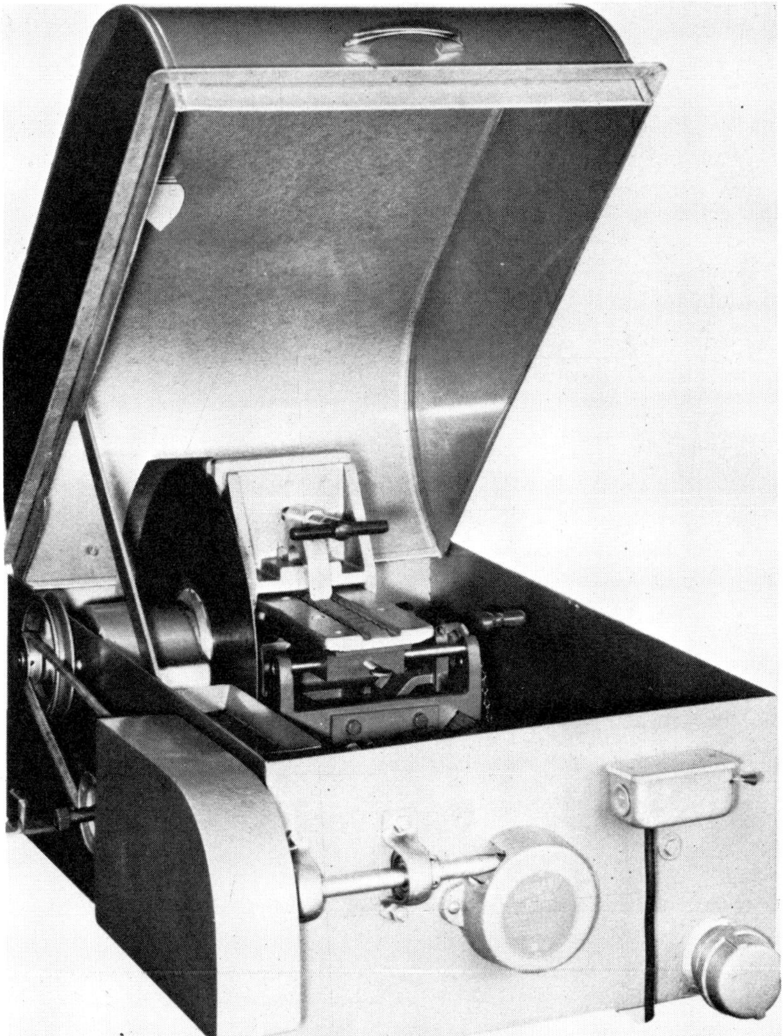

Plate 3   The Highland Park 12-16in slab saw.

how safe the machine is by actually holding his fingers against the 'cutting edge' when the blade is in motion, and not losing a finger.

The cutting action is unlike most other saws in that the blade has no teeth. It is a disc, usually made of steel, with small particles of diamond embedded in the edge. It took many years of development to produce a blade like this which is strong, and cheap enough, for the amateur lapidary. This is one of the advances that has made it possible for the art of lapidary to be enjoyed as a hobby by so many thousands.

Before these saws were perfected the method of cutting stone was to use a soft steel disc 'charged' with an abrasive such as emery or silicon carbide. These abrasives could not be embedded in the steel and had to be applied to the edge of the disc as a thin paste or mud. This would then very gradually grind a groove somewhat wider than the blade—an extremely slow and messy procedure.

There are two main types of blade, both usually made of soft steel, although the smaller ones are often made from bronze or copper.

Notch rim blades
These are the least expensive, but being more robust are the ones used by most amateurs [see figure 1].

The blade is charged by cutting slots around the edge and filling them with a mixture of powdered metal and diamond dust. The edge is then rolled, to close the notches and slightly thicken the edge for clearance. Heat is applied to melt the powdered metal around the diamond dust, then the blade is straightened and trued. The notches are sometimes cut at right angles to the edge, which means the blade can rotate in either direction; or at a slight angle, which means the blade is best turned one way only. It can be an advantage to be able to turn the blade around when the saw is cleaned, as no matter how carefully it is used, it does tend to wear more on one side than the other.

Fig 1 Part of notch rim blade.

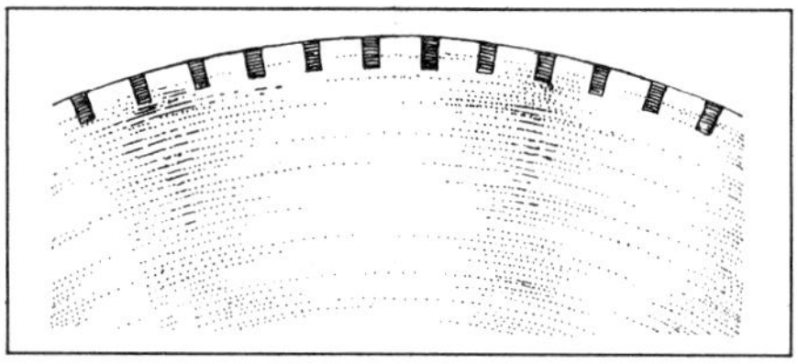

Sintered rim blades
The other type of blade, which gives a much smoother cut, is made by compressing the mixture of powdered metal and diamond dust into a hoop. This is heat treated, or sintered, until the particles fuse. The hoop is then soldered onto the edge

of the steel disc. A variation of this is the segmented sintered rim, where sintered sections are applied separately to the rim. These saws can be rotated in either direction [see figures 2 and 3].

Fig 2 Part of segmented sintered rim blade.

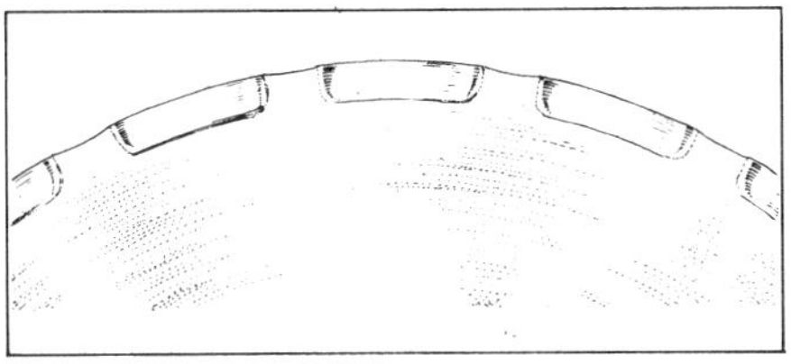

Fig 3 Part of continuous sintered rim blade.

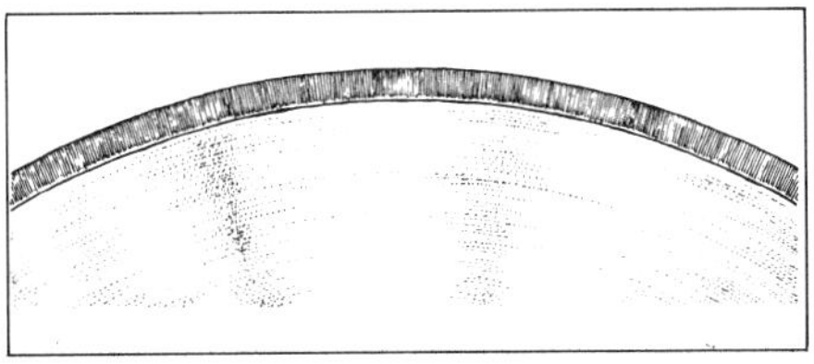

Manufacturers give very precise instructions on the use of their blades and as they are so expensive it is well worthwhile following them. A blade, used properly, can have a very long cutting life, but if misused can be ruined very quickly. All diamond blades cut with the same action; when the stone touches the blade it quickly scrapes away the metal surrounding the diamond which then begins to cut. Sometimes, particularly if a great deal of rock of the same hardness has been cut, the metal tends to be pushed back over the diamond and prevent it cutting. This can be put right by sawing through an old grinding wheel or soft fire brick a few times to grind away the metal and expose the diamond. Cutting rocks of varying hardness will prevent this from occurring.

Shafts and bearings

Diamond blades are expensive, therefore it is important they are mounted in such a way as to give maximum efficiency and long life. Shafts should be thick and stiff enough not to bend or whip. Small blades, up to 8in, need a shaft of at least ½in thick and above this diameter ⅝ to 1in. The threaded end of the shaft, where the blade is mounted, can be thinner providing the remainder is of the correct size.

Blades are always mounted with a flange (a large dished washer) each side. Thinner blades need larger flanges, as much as three-quarters of their diameter being covered; 8 to 10in blades need 1½ to 2½in flanges depending on their thickness.

Shafts must be housed in bearings which allow easy yet accurate running. Several types of bearing are available but the best is a sealed-for-life ball bearing race. These make sure that no stray particles of grit find their way into the bearing with disastrous results.

Rock clamps

It is possible, on any diamond saw, to cut a slice from a piece of rock by holding it in the fingers and feeding it in by hand; however, this causes problems and limitations. The rock must have a reasonably flat surface at right angles to the cut, so that it can be held firmly onto the table. When cutting a large piece by hand it is quite difficult to be certain that the cut is straight.

Fig 4 Method of starting a cut on a sloping surface.

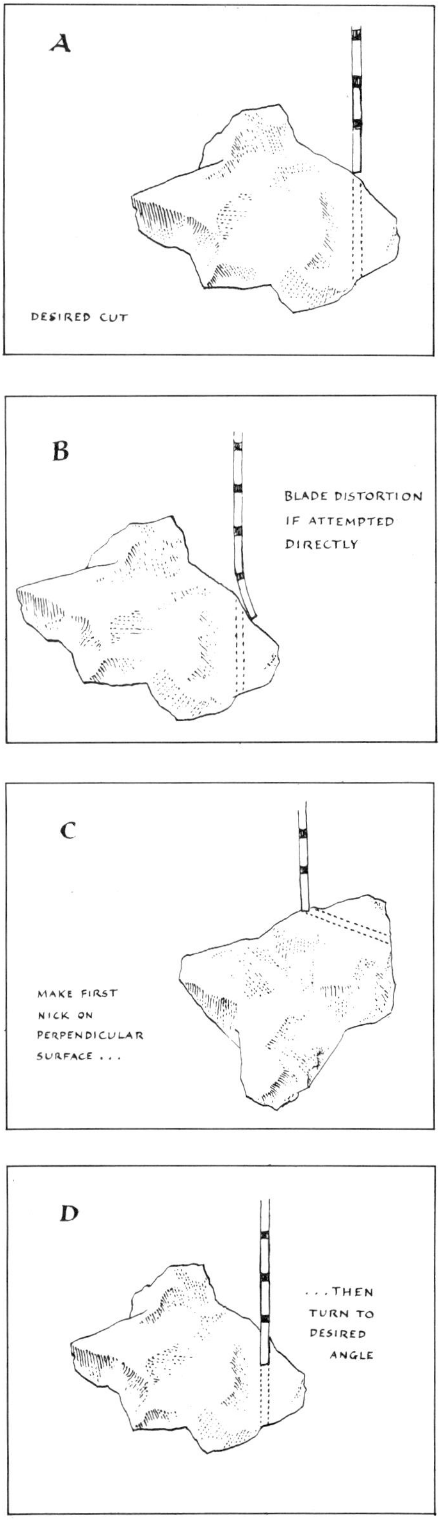

The slightest tilting or twisting of the rock can cause the blade to jam or bend, very often resulting in irreparable damage to the blade. If no rock clamp is available it is worth-while practicing on slices of material until the correct 'feel' and control are established. Ideal slices of marble and feldspar with at least one flat side can often be obtained from the local stonemason or from shop fronts that are being demolished or re-modelled.

Having decided where the first cut is to be made it is important to present the stone to the blade at right angles. If an attempt is made to start the cut on a sloping surface the blade is certain to slide along the slope with the possibility of blade distortion. This can be overcome by making a small nick, with the saw, at right angles to the slope and then gently turning the rock until it is lined up in the direction of the cut.

The rock must be held firmly with both hands, the distance between opposing forefingers and thumbs being very little more than the thickness of the blade. Making sure the rock is held firmly in contact with the table, it is fed gently into the blade. Excess forward pressure must never be used; the blade running hot, or slowing down, or sparks being emitted, are all signs of trying to cut too quickly. Slow feeding always causes far less wear on a blade. Care must also be taken to avoid the last fraction of rock from breaking and leaving a small projection, or nib, which can push the blade to one side.

The next stage is to make another cut parallel to the first to obtain a slice of material of the required thickness. Some form of adjustable fence is useful for holding the rock against, to ensure a parallel cut. Failing this a piece of wood clamped to the table will serve the same purpose.

Most 8 to 10in trim saws, and all slabbing saws, have some form of rock clamp, or vice, which is mounted so that it can slide parallel to the blade, with some system for lateral adjustment to allow for several cuts without altering the position of the rock in the vice.

One of the simplest forms of rock clamp is shown in figure 5.

The weight of the rock, plus the arm, is enough to hold the specimen against the blade whilst cutting. This is the basic idea—all sorts of improvements can be made: a set screw in the arm can be used to prevent the arm dropping at the end of the cut; weights can be added to increase the pressure for smaller

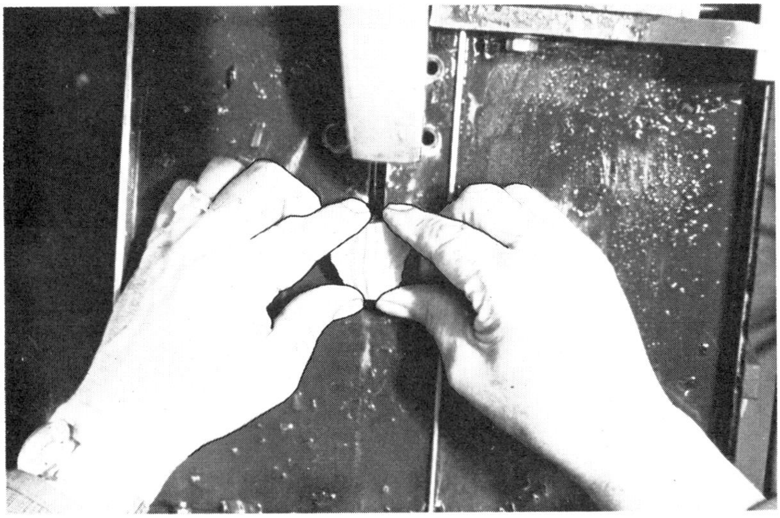

Plate 4 Correct position of thumbs and fingers when cutting without a vice.

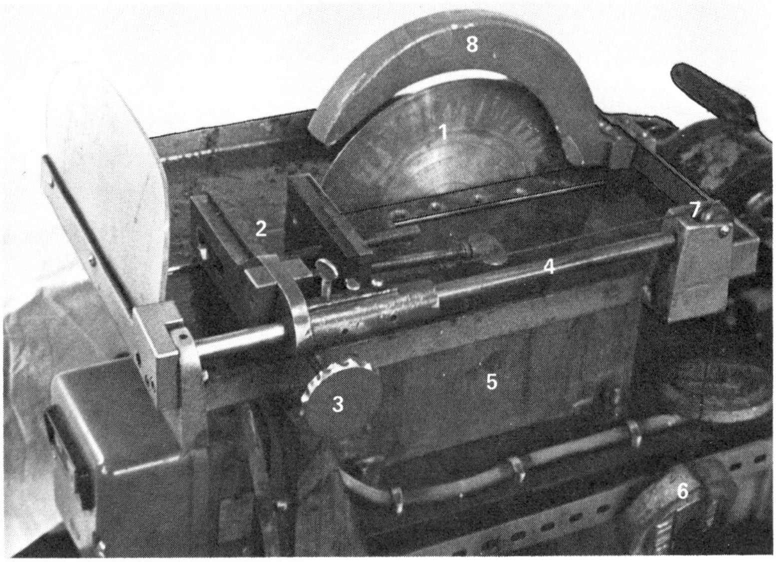

Plate 5 Highland Park 10in trim saw: (1) saw blade and arbor (2) rock clamp or vice (3) cross feed screw (4) guide rod (5) coolant tank (6) weight and wire (7) pulley wheel (8) splash guard.

rocks; and the hinge could be replaced with a rod, a sleeve and a locking device to provide lateral adjustment.

Most clamps are constructed of metal for strength, with the jaws lined with a hard wood which gives a much better grip on the stone.

It is very important to check there is no movement of the stone in the vice while being cut, or it can jam and damage the blade. Ways and means of holding difficult pieces are suggested later in this chapter. An excellent clamping device is shown in Plate 6 consisting of two vertical threaded arms, each with a sleeve connected with a length of chain. This gives a very positive hold, even on very awkward shapes.

Fig 5 Simple gravity feed rock clamp.

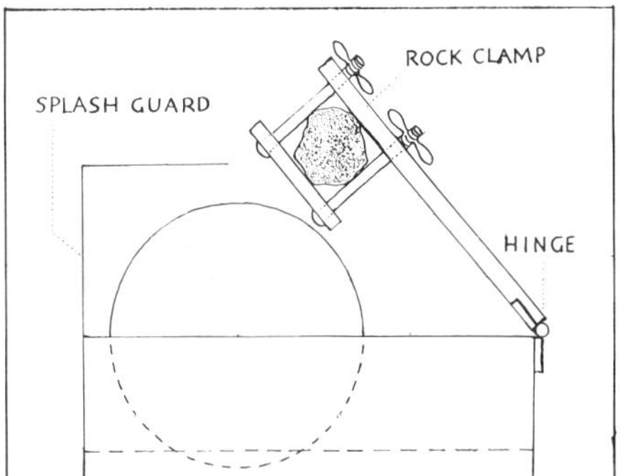

Plate 6 Avon 10in trim saw showing chain rock clamp

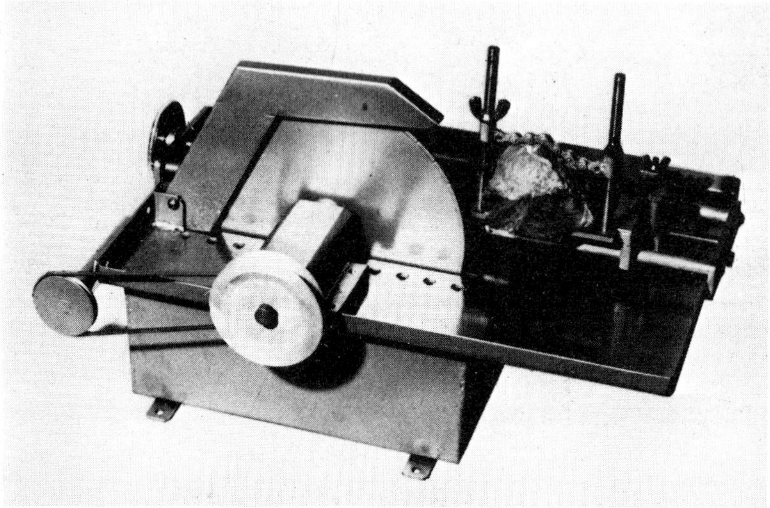

The cross feed can be set up as in Plate 6, which shows a flat plate running in two rebates and locked in position with two wing nuts. Plate 5 shows a different arrangement using a more traditional clamp and a threaded bar for lateral adjustment. Guide rods are used to slide the clamp forward, keeping it parallel to the blade. In Plate 5 one rod is provided and the forward motion is obtained by linking a piece of wire from the clamp, over a small pulley wheel, to a weight.

Opposite: Feldspars, showing (a) sunstone (b) moonstone (c) labradorite (d) laurvikite (e) amazonite; and flat lapped stones, showing (f) forest (or cotham) marble (g) granite.

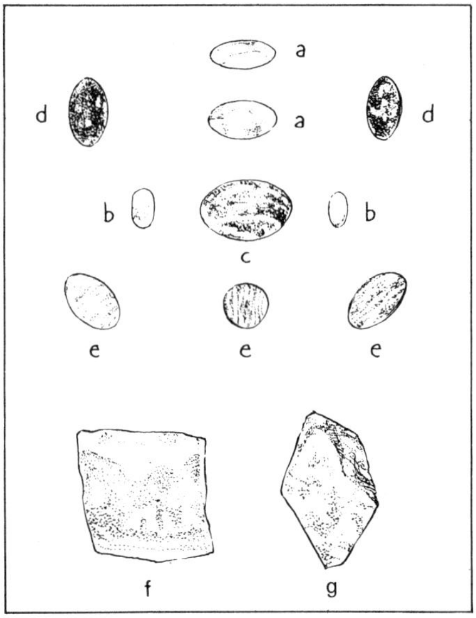

Two guiding rods are shown in Plates 6 and 7 and a long threaded shaft running through a hole at the bottom of the clamp to give a screw feed. This shaft is connected to the motor via a worm screw and a belt. A split nut is locked onto the thread to pull the clamp forward.

There are certain disadvantages with the weight feed system which ought to be explained. The weight should be varied with the thickness, and hardness, of the rock, but most pieces of rough are irregular in shape and the thickness of the section can vary considerably. This means too much pressure at the thin section and too slow a cut at the thick. At the end of the cut the cross section usually narrows very suddenly causing the saw to race through. The slice usually breaks off before the cut is finished, and the weight will pull the clamp very quickly past the blade, causing it to 'ride out' over the nib left on the rock. This may cause the blade to dish or bend.

These disadvantages can be minimised by taking the precaution of feeding the clamp very slowly by hand at the beginning of the cut to make sure the blade does not wander on a sloping surface. The amount of weight can be judged fairly accurately

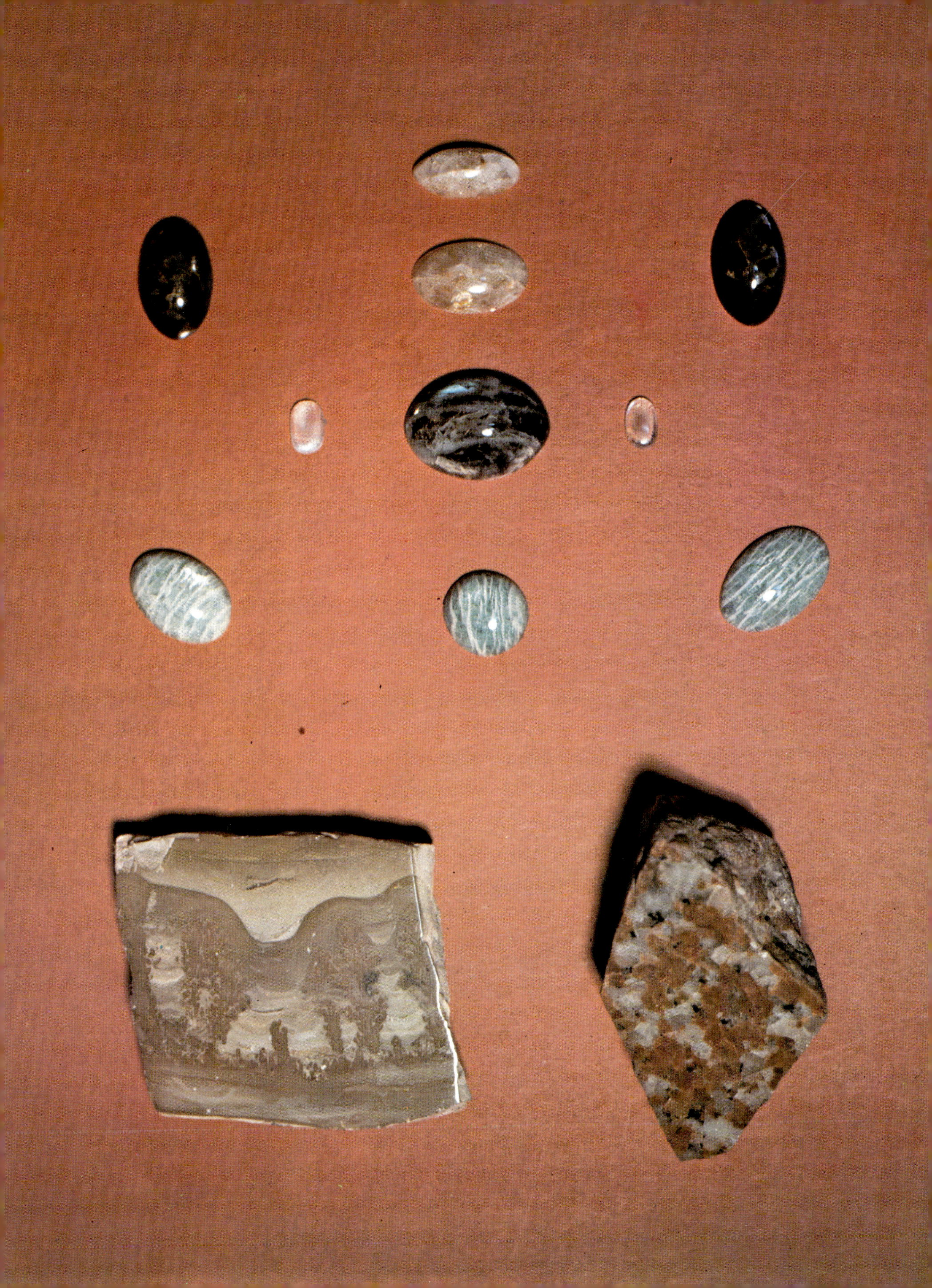

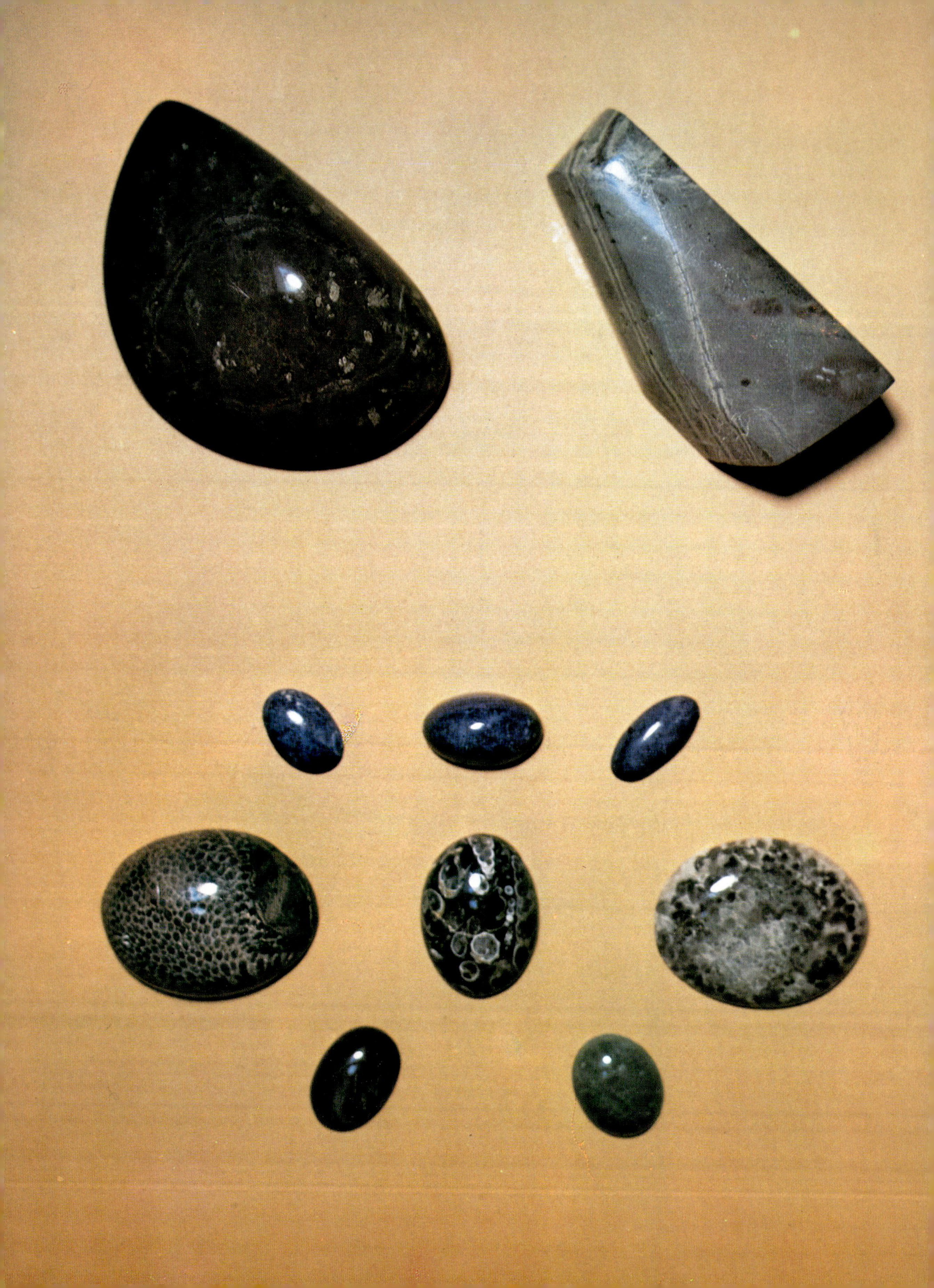

only with experience, but a good guide is to mark a spot close to the beginning of the cut of the average of the thinnest and the thickest parts. Cut to this mark by hand feeding, then add sufficient weights to allow the blade to just continue to cut.

Some system of blocking is needed to stop the clamp just before the end of the cut. This can be done very simply with a piece of wood, cut to the correct length, placed between the clamp and the end of the table. Packing pieces placed underneath the weights to prevent them pulling, or a locking sleeve on the guide

Opposite: Handworked and polished stones, showing (top left) red serpentine and (top right) green serpentine; (a) lapis lazuli (b) fossilised coral (c) turritella agate (d) smoky quartz in milky quartz (e) cat's eye quartz (f) green adventurine.

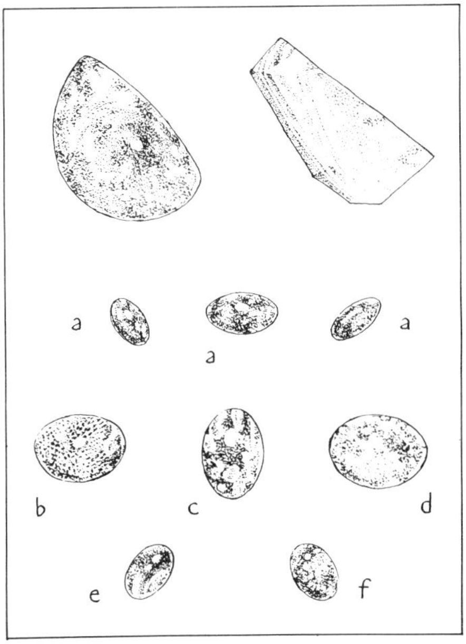

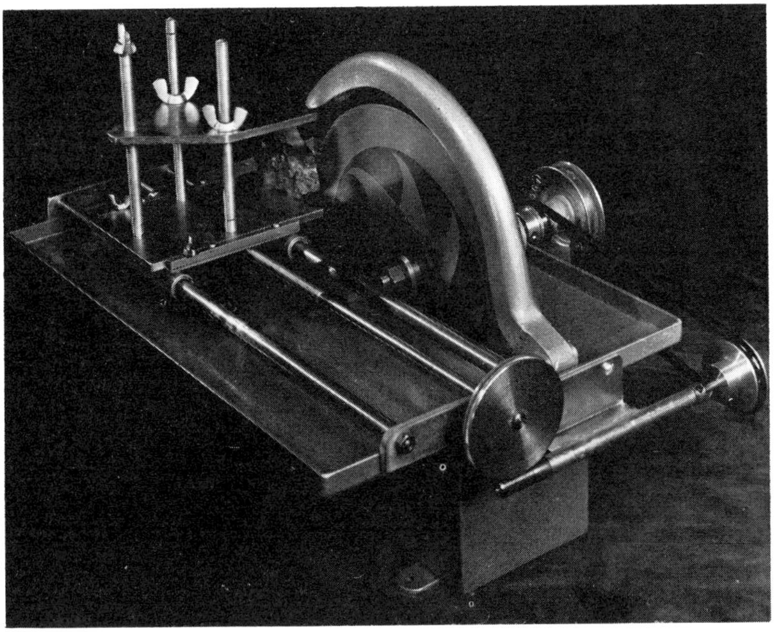

Plate 7 The Kiwi 10in trim saw showing automatic screw feed.

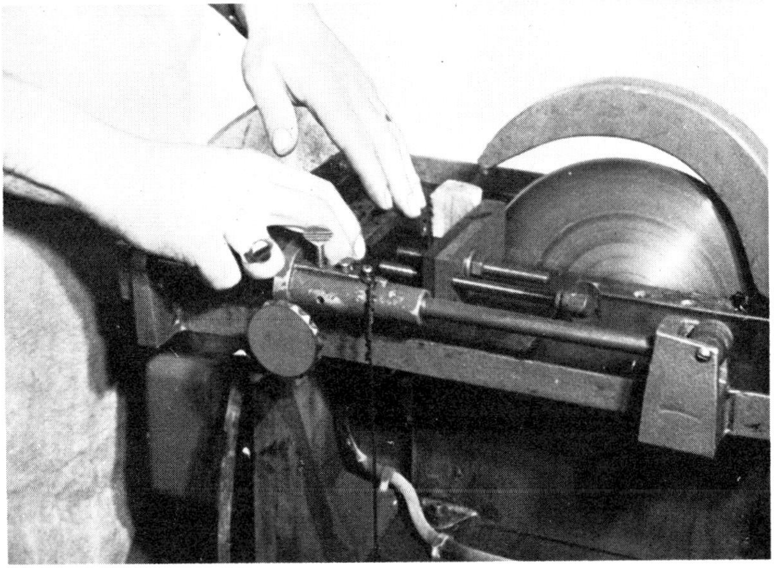

Plate 8 Feeding clamp by hand to start the cut.

rod to halt the clamp at the critical point, are simple solutions. The cut is then carefully finished off by hand feeding. One other disadvantage of the weight feed, that cannot be overcome, is that if the blade is running slightly out of round the bump gets more and more pronounced. The big advantage of the weight feed, of course, is its cheapness with no mechanical parts to give trouble.

Some pieces of rock, due to their peculiar shape, are impossible to hold in any form of clamp. One method of overcoming this problem is to set the piece in plaster of Paris. Use a small cardboard box, just large enough to hold the rock, place the rock in it and level it to the desired position using broken pieces of soft rock. Pour in the mixed plaster and leave to set hard. When it has set, the whole thing, box as well, can be held in the clamp and the saw will cut quite easily through the card, plaster and rock. Setting rocks in plaster is also a useful method of obtaining a flat base for cutting on a small trim saw which has no clamp.

Coolant

Diamond saws should NEVER BE RUN DRY, as tremendous heat is generated, in the blade and the rock, when it is cutting. This heat is dissipated by the use of a liquid coolant contained in a tank beneath the saw table. The bottom ¼in of the blade is allowed to run in the coolant which is then carried around to the cut. Coolant is also used to keep the cut free of stone dust and to act as a lubricant where friction between the blade and stone is set up. Many liquids have been used as a coolant and there are just as many arguments as to which is the best. Transformer oil, flushing oil, diesel oil, and engine oil mixed with paraffin, have been successfully used, but the last two are rather smelly. Soluble oils have some advantages but are not worth using unless it can be guaranteed they will not cause rusting; some of them also tend to increase the cutting time. Anti-freeze has been used but it is very penetrating and some porous stones will absorb it quickly. Since turquoise in particular is very porous and will absorb most oils, soaking it in water for two or three days before cutting will fill the pores in the stone and thus prevent penetration.

A good coolant should have the following properties:

(a) A high flash point, to diminish fire risk.
(b) Good lubricating qualities.
(c) Inability to form a mist or vapour.
(d) Odourless.

Lapidary suppliers who stock saws will always have a supply of suitable oils, but usually only sold in quart tins. Shell Petroleum markets an oil called Macron 'A' which fulfils the above requirements and is sold by the gallon.

Most stones tend to be slightly porous, so it is handy to have a pail filled with a strong detergent solution close to the saw for washing all material as soon as it has been cut.

The coolant tank itself usually supports the rest of the saw machinery and should be strong and rigid. The table should be easy to remove for cleaning, which ought to be done regularly; dirty coolant will result in more rapid wear on the blade. To clean, allow the machine to stand idle for a day before cleaning so the particles will have sunk and formed a sludge. Drain off the clean oil from the top, for re-use, and filter the sludge, either using filter paper or a strong brown paper bag suspended over a container. The material left can then be disposed of in the garbage—*never down the drain.*

If a large hole is drilled in the bottom of the tank the oil and sludge could drain directly into a large container placed underneath the saw. A pump placed near the top of this container could then lift cleaner oil directly onto the top of the blade. A split-level container would allow sludge to settle in one half and clean oil to overflow into the other half where the pump would be situated. This method has two distinct advantages:

(a) Clean oil is always being fed to the cutting edge, which will result in faster cutting and longer blade life as no particles of rock dust will be between the cutting diamond and the rock being cut.

(b) There is no messy task of dismantling the machine for cleaning.

Splash hoods

Whilst the saw is cutting, oil is thrown off the blade, is redirected onto the rock by the splashguard, and sprayed off again in all directions. Some form of covering or hood is therefore very useful to confine the oil to the machine, and should fit inside the table edge to drain the oil back into the tank via the table. A plastic hood that can be seen through is helpful but not essential; wood with plastic sheet lining, or a sheet metal cover, can be made fairly easily, while flat sheets of plastic can be fixed with a lightweight angle iron for the corners.

Saw speeds

Most blade manufacturers give the recommended cutting speed in surface feet per minute (s.f.p.m.), that is, the actual distance a spot on the rim travels in one minute. This is not to be confused with r.p.m. Harder rocks need a slower rim speed of about 2,000 to 2,500 s.f.p.m. and softer rocks can use speeds of up to 8,000 s.f.p.m. Few people cut a great deal of the softer rock therefore it is wiser to have the blade cutting at a slower speed; somewhere between 2,000 and 3,000 s.f.p.m. seems to be the most often used. The smaller the blade the higher the r.p.m. will need to be, to obtain the correct cutting speed. A glance at the table of speeds in the appendix will cover most requirements.

Slabbing

Gemstone in the rough is very rarely a neat, straight-sided shape which will fit easily into the vice; rocks are usually rounded nodules, or uneven masses, which must be clamped very carefully and often, small chips and pieces of softwood are of great value when inserted around the rock to give extra points of support. Once the specimen is clamped, test its firmness by gripping with both hands and trying to move it, and remember to position the rough to obtain as many slices as possible without having to move it in the vice, as it is very difficult to line up for a parallel cut.

If the saw has an automatic feeding device, adjust the clamp by hand until the rock is just clear of the blade, start the motor and lock the drive onto the shaft. Before a new saw is used, spin the blade by hand to make sure it is running true and is picking up oil from the tank. If a weight feed is being used, remember the points already mentioned—feed gently by hand to start the cut, allow the weight to take over, and then finish by hand.

3. GRINDING

Grinding is the second major step in producing a polished gemstone, using a motorised grinding wheel to shape the stone. Many of the harder materials, such as garnet and emery, have been crushed and used as abrasives in lapidary, but silicon carbide is now the main abrasive. This is a very hard material which is formed by heating coke and sand in an electric furnace. On Moh's scale of hardness silicon carbide is given a rating of 9.5, diamond being the only material with a higher rating. This means it can scratch, or grind, all stones with a lower value, even the corundums, which are shown as 9 on the scale. In practice, however, the two are so close in hardness that a silicon carbide grinding wheel would be worn down very rapidly if used on corundum.

Abrasive sizes

When silicon carbide is cooled it is crushed and very carefully graded through a series of vibrating screens of various mesh sizes. These sizes are usually referred to as mesh or grit sizes, and roughly speaking, a 60 mesh screen has 60 holes per linear inch, as 100 mesh has 100 holes to the inch and so on. Therefore the higher the mesh number the finer the grit. The most common sizes used in lapidary for grinding are 60, 80, 100, 120, and 220. When ordering loose grit or grinding wheels this grit number must always be quoted.

Grinding wheels

Silicon carbide grinding wheels are made in a variety of sizes for lapidary, depending on the type of machinery being used. Thickness of wheels range from ½ to 1½in and the diameter from 4 to 8in. The centre hole is made to a standard 1in diameter and plastic inserts are provided to reduce it to the required shaft size.

The wheels are made by mixing the grit with clay and feldspar, moulding to shape and firing in a kiln for several days. This fuses the clay and feldspar around the grit to form a very strong, but open, type of bond which allows water to penetrate and soak the wheel. This is an important feature in the grinding of gemstones, as water must be used to prevent the stone overheating. An open structure is also important in the prevention of clogging or glazing of the wheel. By altering the

Plate 9 Simple home-built grinder with the arbor mounted in a box.

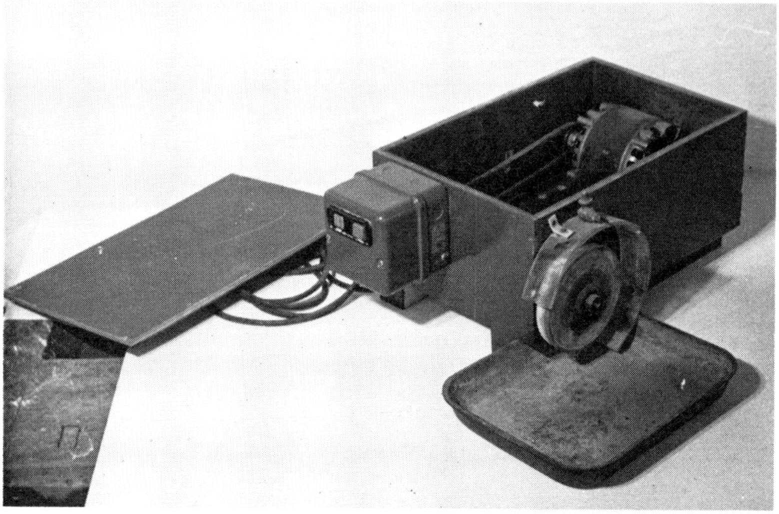

amount of bonding in a wheel, the manufacturer can produce wheels ranging from 'hard' to 'soft'. As a rule, hard wheels are made for grinding softer materials like some metals, and softer wheels for harder materials such as gemstone.

To understand this it must be remembered that the bond merely holds the grit in position to do its work. When the grit becomes blunt it is torn out and exposes new, sharp, particles to continue the work, thus soft bonding allows the particles to be torn out more readily always exposing sharp grit, and a faster cutting action is obtained. Naturally, this means a very rapid wearing down of the wheel, so the lapidary usually compromises by using a medium hard, medium, or medium soft wheel which combines a reasonable grinding speed and wheel life. If grinding wheels are obtained from lapidary dealers the customer can be satisfied he is obtaining the correct softness of wheel.

When ordering grinding wheels it is important to furnish details of diameter and thickness of wheel, grit size, and size of centre hole: many people have been disappointed by the delay caused by neglecting to specify the centre hole size. Only two different wheels are required to do all grinding, a 120 grit wheel being excellent for rough shaping, although some prefer a 100 grit for harder material, and a 220 grit wheel for use on softer material which would be ground away too rapidly to control its shape on a coarser wheel.

Machinery

The simplest form of grinding machine consists of a steel shaft mounted in bearings—sealed-for-life bearings are preferred—

unless they can be well masked from stone dust or loose particles of grit. A very simple construction is shown in Plate 9 with all working parts, except the wheel itself, totally enclosed in a box. An inexpensive shaft with phosphor bronze bearings has been in use for several years on a machine of this type, but it has not been used at full r.p.m.

When two wheels, one coarse and one fine, are to be mounted the layout should be as shown in Plate 10—the wheels at opposite ends of the shaft with the bearings just inside them and the pulley between.

Each wheel should be housed in a trough which must extend far enough in front of the wheel so the water thrown off will end up in the trough instead of soaking the operator.

Plate 10 Rock Rascal double ended 6in grinder.

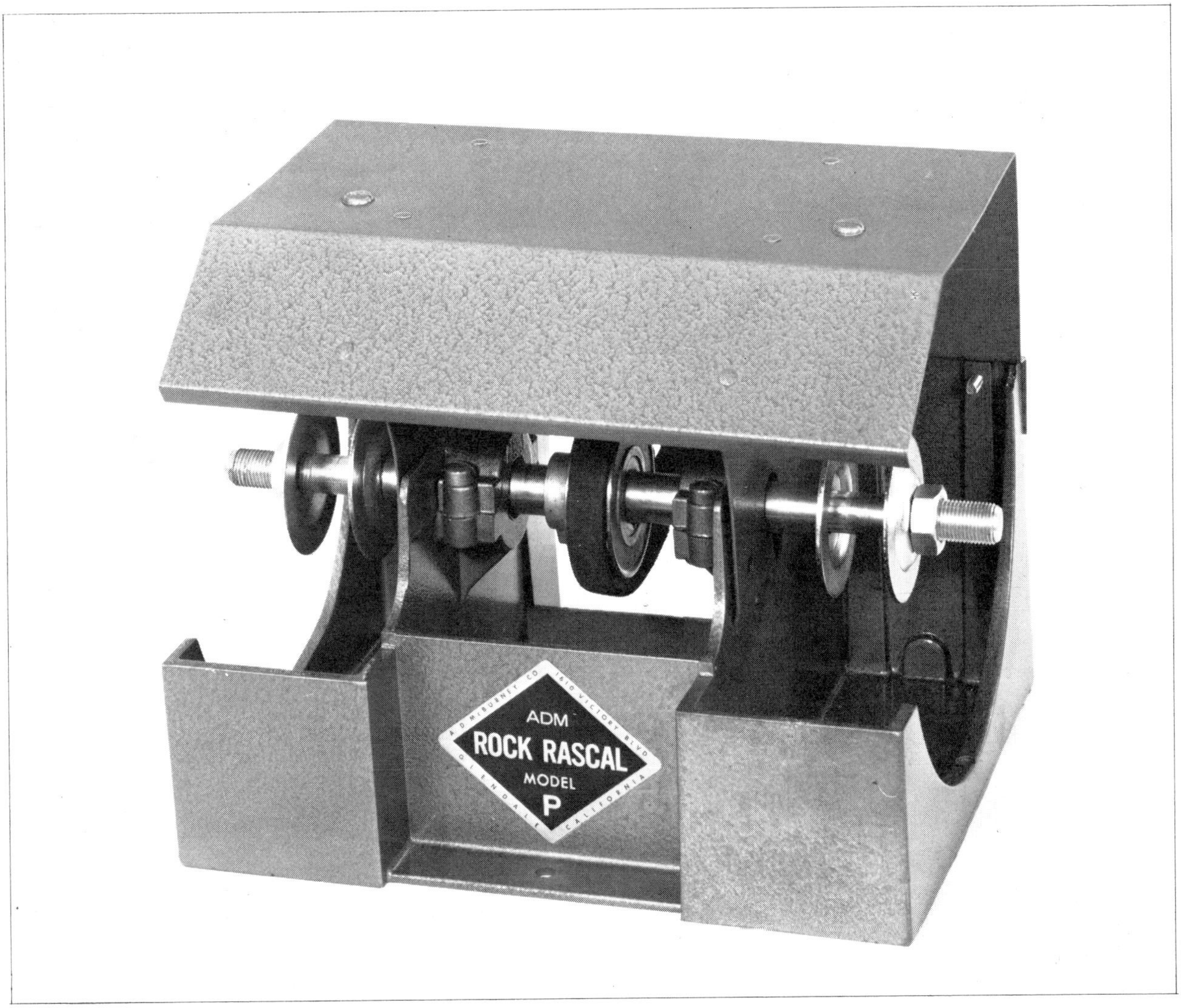

Plate 11 Home-built single grinder.

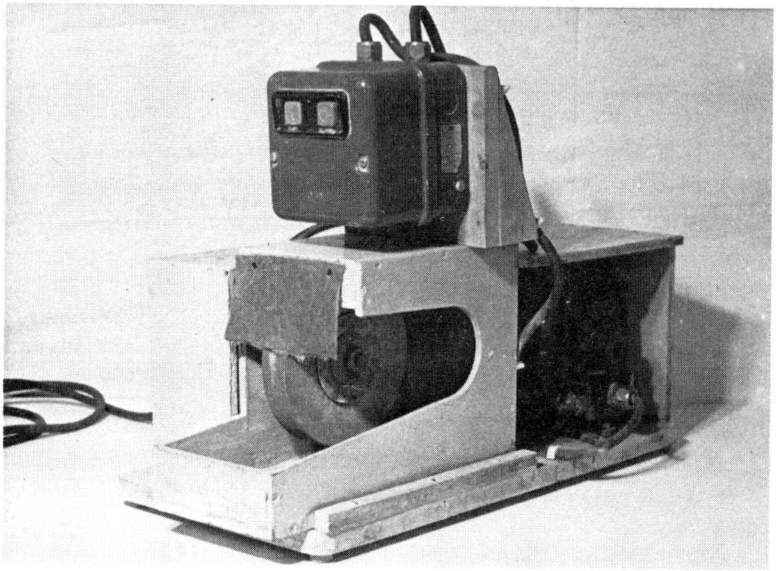

Fig 6 Position of wheels and bearings.

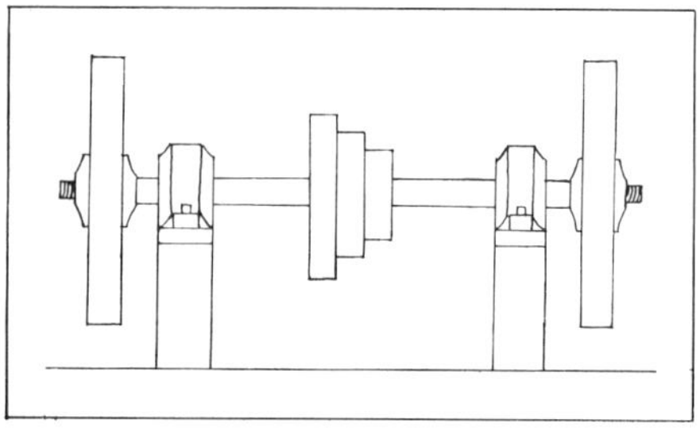

The home-built machine shown in Plate 11 is made of plywood glued and screwed together. All wooden parts are painted with two coats of a waterproof glue and finished with polyurethane gloss. To date this and a similar machine sealed with plastic resin instead of glue, have given five years of continuous use only needing one further coat of paint.

Splash hoods are essential for each wheel, the front of the hood coming far enough down over the wheel to prevent water being thrown at the operator. Although the risk of wheel breakage is very low, the hood should be strong enough to offer some protection against this.

If space permits, it is best to have a separate machine for grinding as shown in Plates 10 and 11. Most amateurs, however, have limited working area and capital, so usually invest in a combination machine like the one shown in Plate 12. All the steps in cutting and polishing a gemstone can be done on this one machine.

So far, only those machines with the wheels mounted vertically have been mentioned, but nearly as popular are those where the wheel is mounted horizontally, as in Plates 13 and 14. The vertical shaft passes down through a splash pan and a sealed bearing which is attached to the underside. The top of the shaft carries the flanges, wheel, and locking nut.

One disadvantage of this arrangement is the single bearing mounted between the pulley and the wheel. The tendency is for

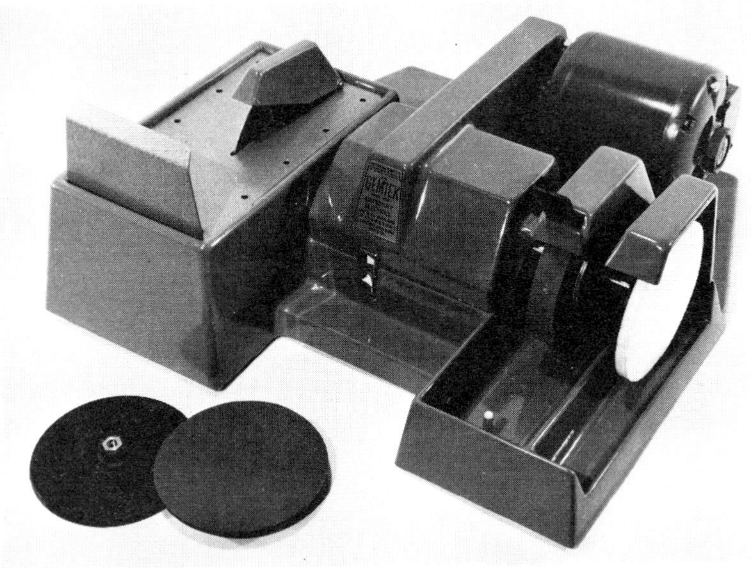

Plate 12 The Gemtek 6in combination machine.

Fig 7 Flange.

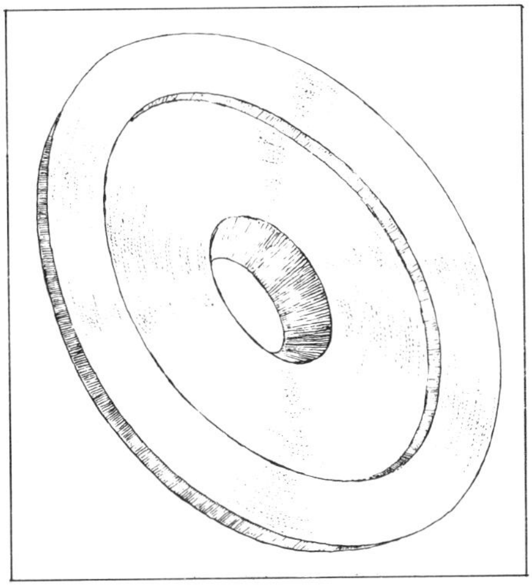

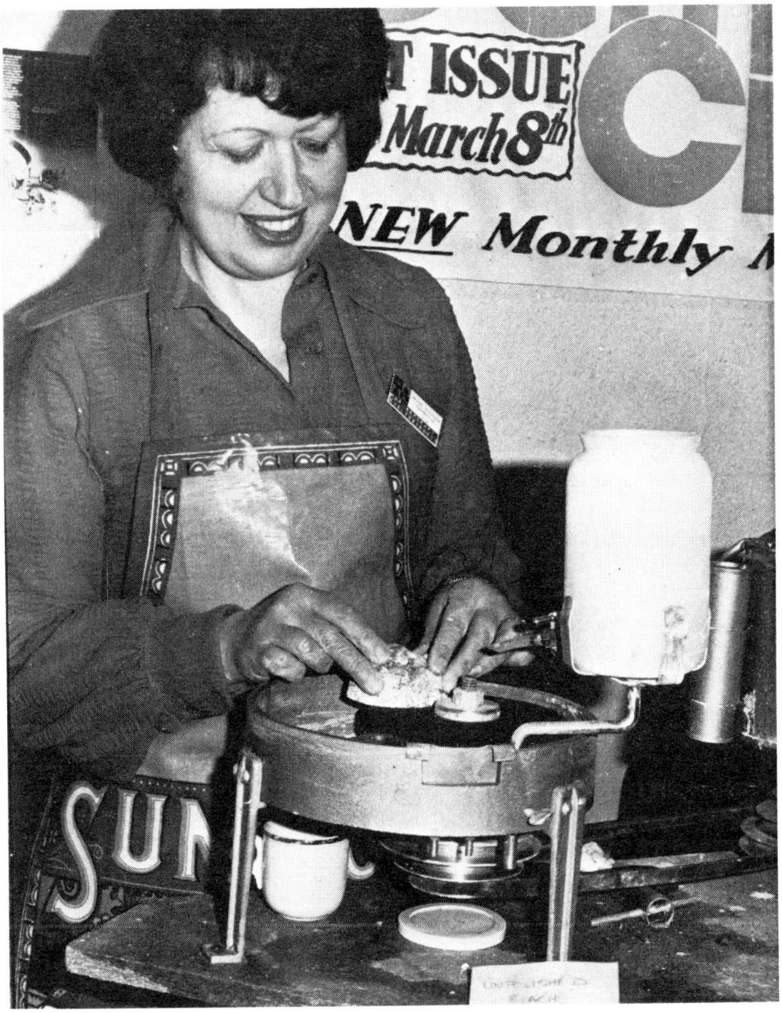

Plate 13 Vertical shaft Robilt being used for grinding.

Plate 14 Robilt 6in Gem-maker showing the edge of the wheel being used for grinding.

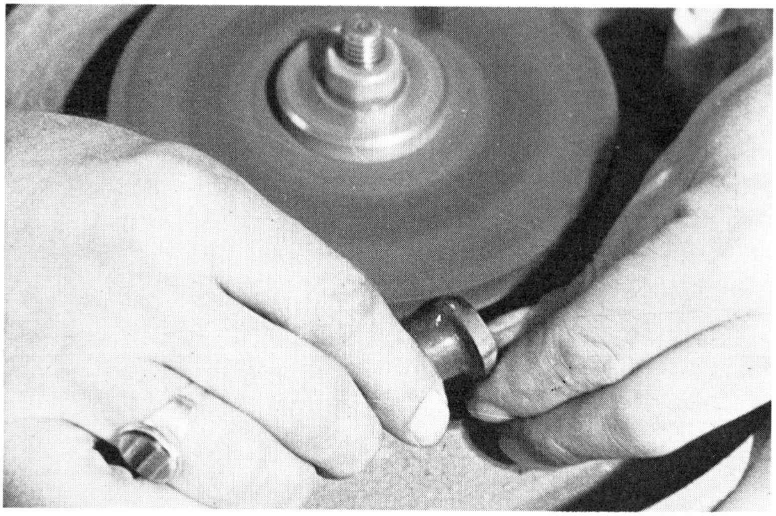

the V-belt to pull the shaft out of line. An improvement to this type of set-up would be a second bearing, preferably self aligning, at the bottom of the shaft. When the pan is large enough to take both hands the edge of the wheel can be used, which means that the point of contact of the stone on the wheel is in full view and affords greater accuracy in grinding. If there is insufficient space then the top—actually the side— of the wheel has to be used instead. This slows down the grinding action and unfortunately it is virtually impossible to true the surface of the wheel.

Grinding wheels must spin at high speed to cut well, therefore the shafts and bearings must be rigid with minimum vibration. The shaft used for a 6in wheel must be at least ½in diameter, and ⅝in for an 8in wheel. The ends of the shaft are threaded to take the nuts, and flanges must be used on each side of the wheel. The shape of these flanges is important—the inside centre portion is cut away to leave a narrow rim which grips the wheel.

If ordinary washers were used the greatest pressure would be on a small area immediately under the nut which could cause the wheel to crack. Care must always be taken when fitting the flanges to make sure no particles of grit are trapped underneath to cause uneven tightening onto the wheel.

Grinding wheel speeds

To get the best results from a grinding wheel it is important to use the correct speed. If the wheel is spinning too fast the particles of grit fly past the stone so quickly their sharp corners are knocked off before they have a chance to cut the gemstone.

In fact if the stone is a hard one, such as agate, the gem actually cuts away the wheel. If the speed of the wheel is too slow the grit hits the stone with less than the required force to cut well. The tendency then is to press harder which results in the grit being torn out and once again a rapid wearing of the wheel. Most authorities agree that the best cutting action is obtained by using a surface speed of between 4,000 and 6,000 feet per minute. All manufacturers label their wheels with the maximum safe speed, and although for safety reasons they have been tested at higher revolutions, it is essential not to exceed the recommended maximum. For a 6in wheel an arbor speed of between 2,500 and 3,000 r.p.m., giving an s.f.p.m. of approximately 4,000 to 5,000, cuts very well and is below the recommended maximum of something over 4,000 r.p.m.

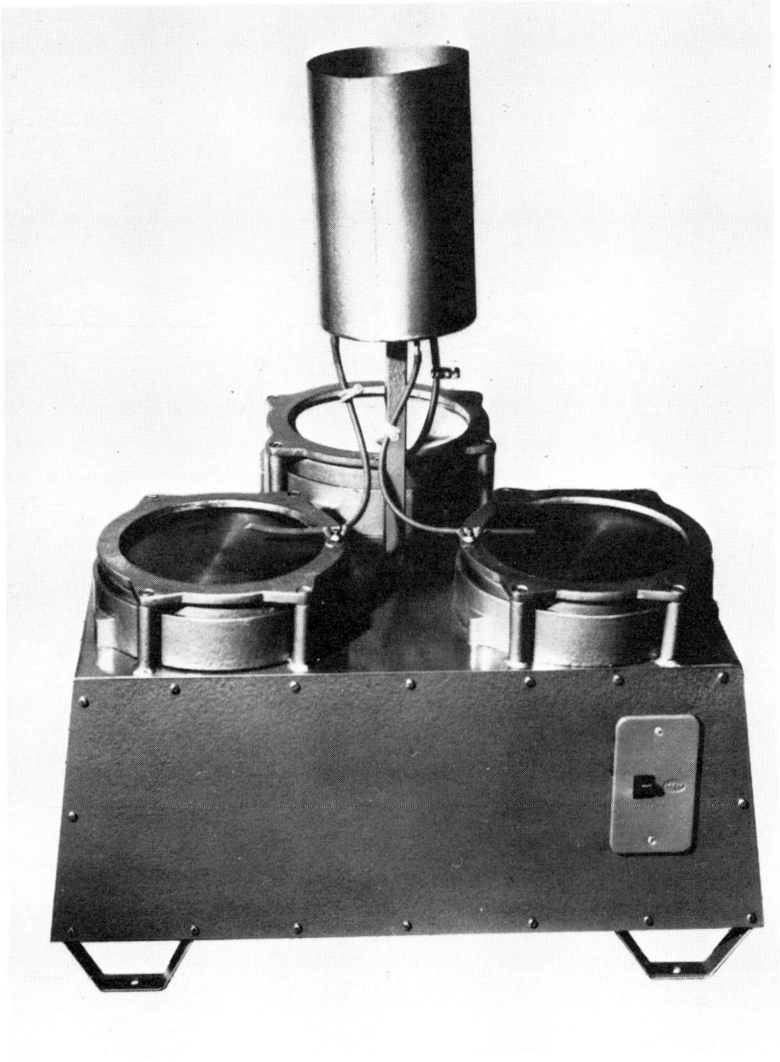

Plate 15 Avon triple head machine for grinding, lapping, sanding, polishing.

Water supply
As has been stressed, an adequate supply of water must reach the grinding wheel when in use, to prevent the gemstone from overheating and to stop the wheel from clogging up with stone dust: equally important one must ensure that no water is in contact with a stationary wheel. This last point must be emphasised, as the wheel, being porous, will quickly absorb water. If it is then rotated at high speed when one half is saturated and completely out of balance, it could shatter.

There are several ways of applying water to the wheel in use. A tube let into a hole in the hood will give a drip or spray onto the wheel, depending on the source of the water. A drip feed is not too successful because it can be applied only to one part of the cutting face. A spray can be made by sealing one end of a tube, bending it at right angles to the wheel, and drilling four or five very small holes in the tube; the tube must then be connected to a water supply that has sufficient pressure to force the water through the small holes. Unfortunately, most work is done in garages or sheds that have no mains supply. The source of water then, is usually from a large can resting as high as possible on a shelf with tubing leading to the machine, and unless the can is placed many feet above the machine there is insufficient pressure to activate a spray.

Another method often used is to pour water into the trough until it is just below the bottom of the wheel. Switch on the machine, place a sponge in the water and move it forward until it is just touching the grinding wheel, when sufficient water is wiped off to wet it. Care must be taken when moving the sponge as if it is pushed too hard onto the wheel it will be picked up, taken around and, if there is enough space beneath the hood, thrown at the operator, who will, as can be imagined, get quite a soaking. When the space between hood and wheel is small, the results can be more disastrous, particularly if no overload switch is fitted. The sponge will jam, stop the machine and probably burn out the motor.

A good supply of water is essential, but an over-generous one can be uncomfortable for the operator. Adjust the supply until a fine spray can be seen coming from the wheel, start grinding and if the wheel turns whitish increase the supply until this whiteness disappears. At this point the importance of electrical connections and wiring must be stressed. If the machine is home built it is always wise to get everything checked by a qualified electrician before use. Water plus faulty or incorrect wiring can be lethal. Motors and switches are best mounted behind the equipment, thus preventing them from being sprayed with water. Portable drills, mounted in bench stands, can be used for small grinding work, but adequate provision must be made to stop spray from getting at the switch and motor. The standard version of most commercial machines is priced without any form of switch, and although it will increase the cost by several pounds it is advisable to have one fitted. Lapidary suppliers will probably be able to supply an overload switch suitable for the job. An electric motor is an expensive item and an overload switch can prevent over working it.

Wheel dressing

Free hand grinding, however carefully done, will eventually cause a slight 'chattering' of the stone against the grinding wheel. This will become more pronounced until there is a definite bumping caused by the wheel wearing out of true; this is accentuated by using too much pressure, particularly when grinding harder stones. The onset of bumping can be retarded by holding the stone very firmly in the fingers, and large stones should not be ground on a small wheel as this will very quickly cause uneven wear and bumping.

As soon as bumping is felt the wheel should be trued, or dressed; the best way of doing this is to use a standard grinding wheel dressing tool of either the star wheel or diamond pattern. The former can be purchased quite cheaply and should be one of the first extras obtained.

A board needs to be clamped horizontally to the trough so that the top is just below shaft height. The dressing tool is held firmly against the leading edge and moved lightly back and forth across the face of the revolving wheel as shown in Plate 16. Turn on the water supply when doing this to keep down the dust. The star-shaped wheels turn and tear out the higher spots, gradually levelling the grinding wheel.

Another form of uneven wear more likely to be caused by the beginner than by the experienced lapidary, is the hollowing of the face of the wheel. This is caused by grinding on the centre of the face instead of using the whole of it. A wheel dresser can be used to flatten the face but it does waste a lot of grinding wheel, so one should always keep available a few pieces of agate that need grinding, putting these to the higher edges of the face to bring it level again.

Plate 16 Star wheel grinding wheel dresser in use for truing the wheel.

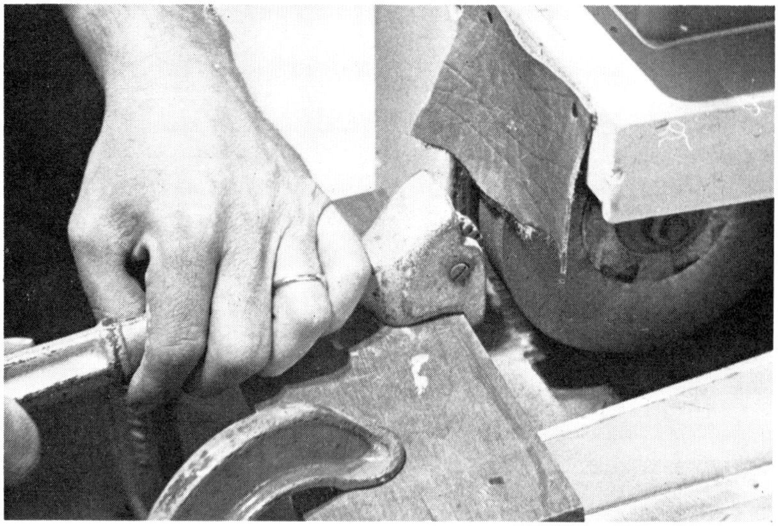

Plate 17 Holding fingers against wet grinding wheel.

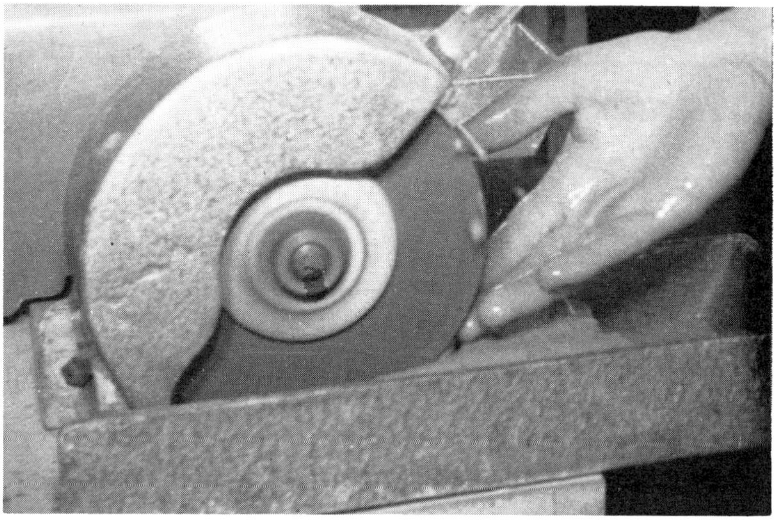

Plate 18 Position of thumbs and fingers for holding stone for grinding. Note hands resting on trough for support.

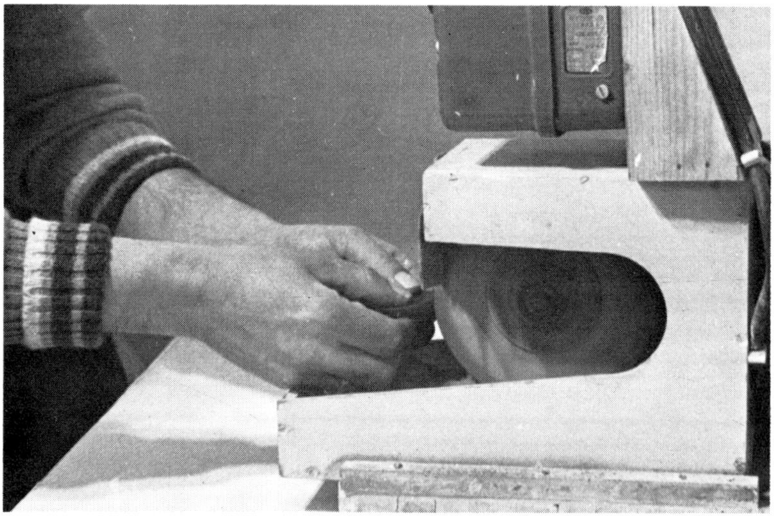

Correct use of grinding wheels

It is essential, right from the beginning, to use the following procedure when grinding:

(a) switch on;
(b) turn on the water, or adjust sponge;
(c) grind;
(d) turn off water, or remove sponge;
(e) allow wheel to spin for a few moments to dry out;
(f) switch off.

When installing a new grinding wheel suspend it between thumb and forefinger before putting it on the arbor. Tap it gently with a small piece of wood—it should ring with a clear note, if a dull thud is heard it probably means a hidden crack and the wheel should not be used.

Place the wheel on the arbor, remembering the precautions already mentioned concerning flanges and over-tightening. Spin the wheel by hand to make sure that it is running true—stand to one side—just in case—and switch on, leaving it running for a few minutes. Some people may be a little nervous of a high speed grinding wheel at this stage, so with plenty of water on the wheel and the palm facing upwards, lightly brush the finger tips against the face of the wheel as shown in Plate 17.

All that will be felt is a slight tickling sensation, but remember to make sure the wheel is wet and never attempt this with a dry wheel otherwise the fingers will be burned by friction.

Select a piece of rock, preferably a sawed slab approximately 1½in diameter and about $\frac{3}{16}$ to ¼in thick. Hold the stone as shown in Plate 18, thumbs on top, fingers underneath close to the front edge.

The position in which the rock is held in relation to the wheel is important. If it is too high above the centre it may be snatched out of the hands and also cause nicks on the wheel face, while holding the rock too low makes it difficult to grind at right angles to the bottom, which is necessary to obtain a correct shape. The best position is level with the shaft.

The work must be adequately supported otherwise it will soon begin to chatter against the wheel and before long will bump quite severely. Work rests are available on some machines but unless these are adjustable and easily removed they can get in the way when grinding a curved surface, as the hands must move freely to create the desired shape. If a work rest is used it

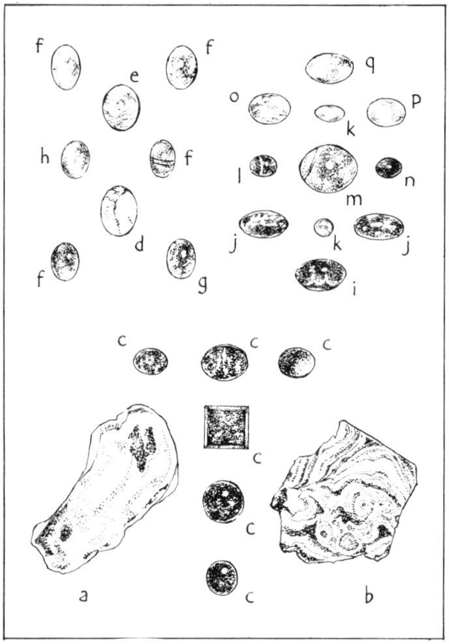

Opposite: (a) Indian agate (b) malachite (c) bloodstone (d) moss agate (e) rutilated quartz (f) carnelian (g) amethyst (h) citrine (i) tiger eye (j) jasper (k) opal doublet (l) blue tiger eye (falcon's eye) (m) serpentine (n) chalcedony (o) moss opal (p) amber (q) chrysophrase.

must always be kept as close as possible to the wheel to prevent the stone getting jammed in between. Adequate support is made possible by resting the wrists or sides of the hands on the water trough.

Holding the slab firmly, slowly advance the work to the wheel and move it across the face aiming to grind a gentle curve and keep the side at right angles to the bottom. Do not jam sharp corners into the wheel otherwise pitting and then bumping will occur.

Examine the edge frequently to see what is happening. At first it will be difficult to replace the stone at the same angle to the wheel and many different faces will be ground. Practice this until a single continuous surface is formed, and try the exercise several times with rocks of differing hardness to get the feel of the grinding action. Sometimes, small chips are broken off from the bottom edge; if this occurs grind a very small bevel, at about 45 degrees, along the bottom edge.

When the above technique has been mastered try the following exercises:

(a) with a piece of aluminium rod sharpened to a point, draw a curved line and grind accurately to it;
(b) try the above exercise on different rocks using a tighter curve each time;
(c) mark out a complete circle and grind to the line;
(d) using small pieces, about ½ to ¾ in diameter, repeat (a), (b) and (c);
(e) take a piece about 1 in across and grind one side straight;
(f) mark a right angle and grind the corner square.

Few beginners will probably have sufficient patience to take all of these steps before trying their hand at grinding a cabochon, but it is worth remembering that a gem shape is created by the grinding process and that 'practice makes perfect'.

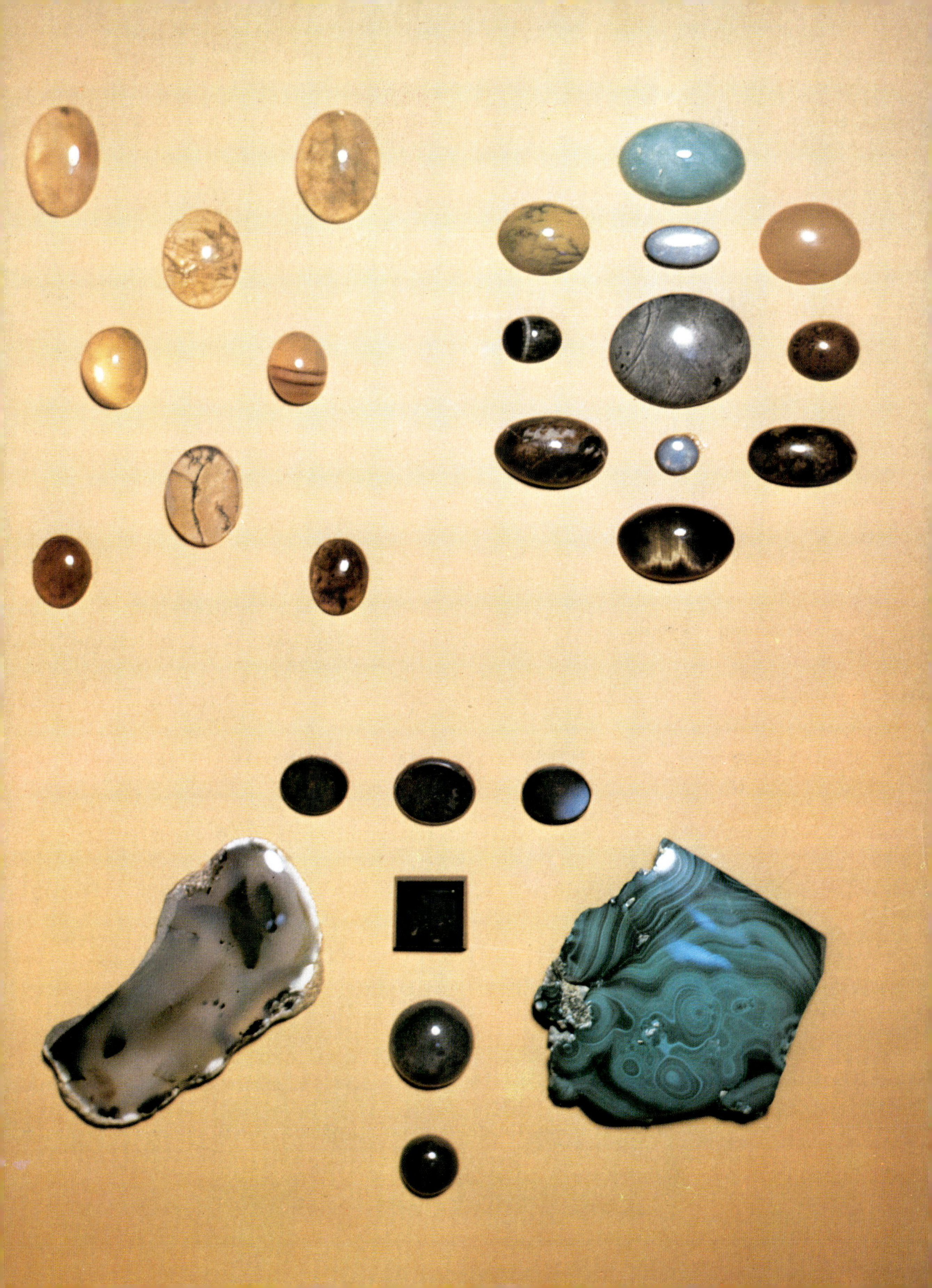

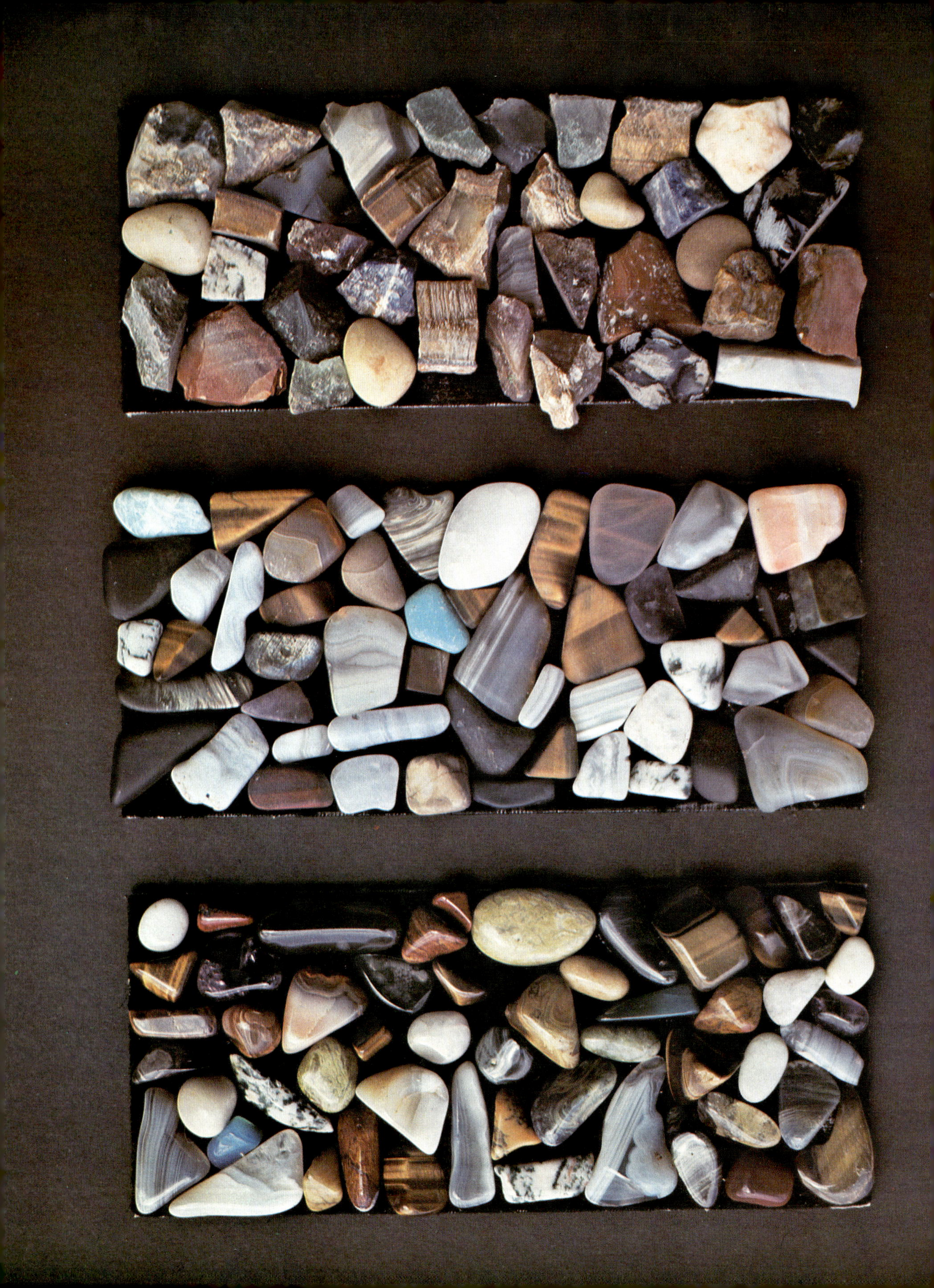

4. SANDING

Sanding is the final and most important stage before polishing and is used mainly on curved surfaces. It can even replace the grinding wheel for shaping small, very soft, stones which would be cut too rapidly by grinding. If the correct equipment is available it can also be used in place of fine lapping, as discussed in a later chapter.

What is sanding?

All materials being prepared to take a high polish must have all scratches and marks removed to leave a very fine surface. When sanding a gemstone, progressively finer abrasives are used to remove marks left by the coarser grits.

Sanding, in lapidary, usually means the use of a suitable abrasive cemented to a flexible material such as paper or cloth. For speed and efficiency the cloth or paper is fixed to a rotating wheel. Flexibility is important as no matter how carefully the stone has been ground it is always covered with flat spots left by the grinding wheel, which the flexible sander removes to give a smooth curve.

Abrasives

Silicon carbide is again the main abrasive used for the sanding operation. Diamond dust can be employed, but is so expensive it is reserved for the very hard costly stones. Grit sizes are finer than those in grinding, 220, 320, 400, 500 and 600 being used most otten. These can be used either as loose grit applied to a 'carrier' such as wood or leather, or bonded to a paper or cloth backing in the form of sheet, disc, strip or belt. The cheapest form of backing is paper, sold as discs or in sheets of 'wet and dry' paper as used for rubbing down cars after spraying. Although the circles overlap slightly, it is cheaper to cut two 6in discs from an 11in × 9in sheet than to buy them ready cut. Cloth backed abrasives are far more expensive but have a much longer life; paper backing tends to tear well before the abrasive is worn out, thus cloth is used for strip and belts where more strain is put onto it. Strip is relatively cheap compared with discs but this is usually offset by the larger quantity in which it is sold.

Sanding machines

All types of sanders, except the belt sander, can be set up as

Opposite: Tumbling, showing (top) rough stone, (centre) first grind, (bottom) polished stone.

Fig 8 Layout for grinder-sander.

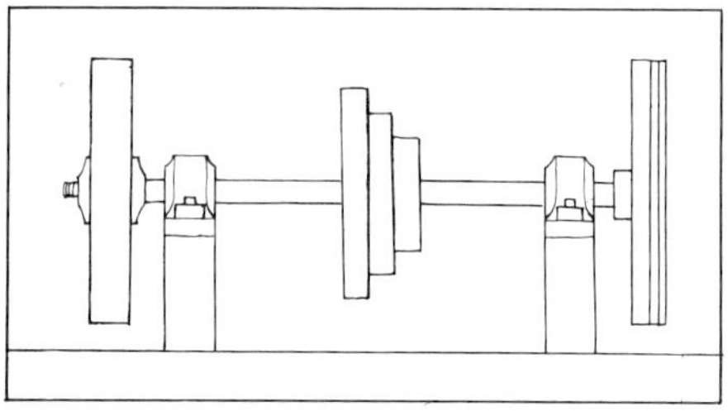

part of a combination machine. The sanding arrangement is usually found at the right hand end of the shaft [see Plate 19], which can prove to be awkward for a left-handed person who would be well advised either to make his own machine, or think in terms of a drum sander.

The arbor, bearings and mountings should have the same characteristics as the grinding machines already mentioned; a suggested layout is shown in figure 8. This is the same as the double grinder shown previously with a sanding disc replacing one of the wheels.

Disc sanders

Disc sanding machines are by far the cheapest to make or buy and will therefore be dealt with in more detail.

Discs can be used quite successfully on both vertical and horizontal shafts, with two main recognised ways of attaching the discs to the machine: the first uses a plywood wheel cut to the same diameter as the abrasive disc. A piece of rubber is cemented to it to allow the disc to conform to the curve of the stone. Soft foam rubber will follow the shape on a steep curve better but is easily torn and will wrinkle the disc quickly, particularly a paper one, and while hard rubber is best used on shallow curves it makes it more difficult to remove small 'flats', thus an ideal compromise is carpet underlay which has the correct amount of resilience for most shapes. The underlay is cemented to the plywood, canvas side down, and to protect the softer rubber a piece of fine canvas is glued onto it. Any contact adhesive can be used for both these joints. The disc itself is held by a 'peel-em-off' adhesive—a non-hardening glue that usually makes replacement a very simple task. However, a fine paper disc can occasionally be difficult to remove. To overcome this, press a piece of agate fairly hard against the revolving disc without using water. The cement is heated up and the disc should then be easily peeled off. A hole, the same size as the threaded shaft, passes through the disc, rubber and plywood, which are then placed onto the machine with a flange each side in the same way as a grinding wheel. The main disadvantage of this arrangement is that the centre 2 or 3in of the disc cannot be used because of the flanges.

It is useful to have at least one plywood disc without rubber for sanding flat surfaces on softer stones.

The second method of attaching a disc is to use a casting of aluminium alloy with a tapped boss [see Plate 20] which is screwed onto the end of the shaft. The rubber is glued to the face, and the disc to the rubber, with the obvious advantage of being able to use the whole disc. It is more convenient to have at least three of these castings, one each for coarse, fine and medium discs.

Another system is used on the sander shown in Plate 21. This calls for a casting to be made, three locating holes to be drilled and three locking slots cut. The main advantage here is that any number of plywood wheels, having the three screws set correctly in the back, can be interchanged very easily.

The life of sanding discs can be prolonged by brushing in a circular motion with warm water, working from the centre. This tends to move unused particles of grit from the centre portion,

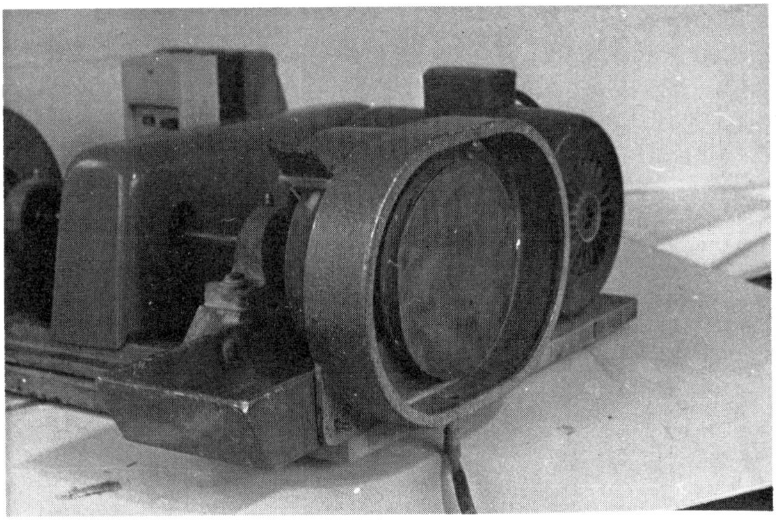

Plate 19 Gemtek double grinder showing sanding attachments.

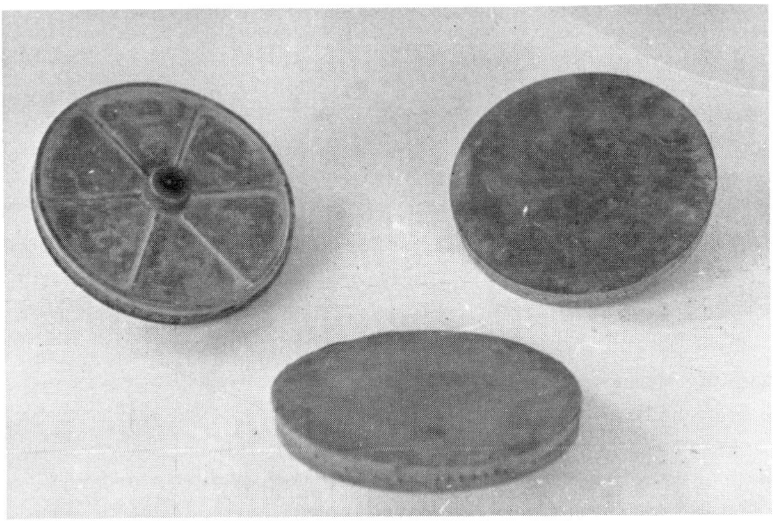

Plate 20 One type of aluminium cast backing for discs.

Plate 21 Casting to take interchangeable plywood wheels.

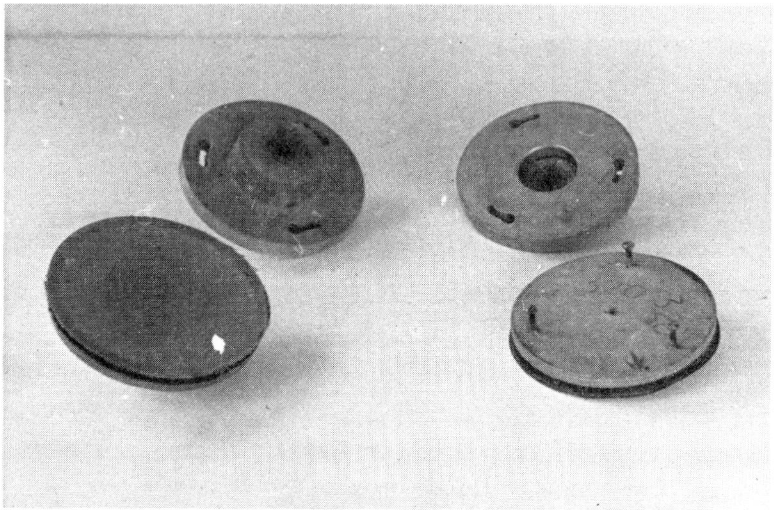

which moves too slowly to be used much, and rolls the grit nearer the edge to expose sharper corners. The disc needs to be left to dry thoroughly before re-using.

Wooden wheels

The wood used to make these wheels should be the type where there is very little difference between the winter and summer growth, i.e. no pronounced annual rings. Mahogany, obeche and holly are timbers that have been used successfully. The wheels, 1½ to 2in thick, need to be turned on a lathe and various curves cut in the rim or side, depending whether it is used horizontally or vertically. A groove, the nearest shape to the curve being sanded, is chosen and a mixture of grit and water is put into it. Very firm pressure is needed to begin cutting and to embed the grit in the wood. As plenty of water is needed to avoid overheating the stone, the wheel should be soaked in hot paraffin wax to impregnate it and prevent water absorption and subsequent warping.

Leather discs

Discs of thin leather cemented onto soft felt or rubber also make useful sanders, particularly on stones that undercut badly. Loose grit mixed with water is applied to the surface. Sufficient water is used to keep the gem cool but if too much is used the stone slides on the wet leather. Coarse, medium and fine sanding can be done on leather but it is very much slower than using wet and dry discs.

All the discs mentioned can be used on either horizontal or vertical shafts.

Drum sanding

There are two main types of drum sander. The first [see figure 9] consists of a metal drum covered with a sponge rubber cushion. A slot is provided for inserting the ends of the cloth strip and a locking bar inside to hold the cloth in place. This type of drum can revolve at high speed providing it is well balanced. The other type of drum is an inflatable rubber wheel using an endless cloth belt which is slipped over when deflated. The resilience of this drum can be altered by a change of pressure.

Belt sanding

The belt sander needs to be constructed as a separate machine, the basic requirement being an endless belt over two rubber-faced rollers as shown in figure 10. Between the rollers where the cloth is unsupported, it yields and conforms to the rounded shape of the stone; it is also possible to arrange a backplate between the rollers so that flat surfaces can easily be sanded.

Although a belt sanding machine is very versatile, it is probably the most difficult to make and the most expensive to buy.

Sanding speeds

Sanding has a similar cutting action to grinding and the same speed, in s.f.p.m., is applicable. It must be remembered on disc sanders that the speed is calculated for the edge of the disc and it reduces rapidly towards the centre. Exceptions to the high speed used for sanding are the wooden wheel and the leather disc, which have to be used much slower, between 400 and 750 r.p.m. if the loose grit is not to be thrown off.

A high-speed sanding machine is useful because the cutting action is faster, therefore lighter pressure can be used which makes it easier for the beginner to move the stone rapidly and avoid cutting flat surfaces. High speed also reduces the tendency some gemstones have to undercut. Many gemstones are uniform in structure and can be sanded in any direction, while others have decided differences in structure which cause them to be weaker in certain directions and show hard and soft spots. Some have two or more minerals with varying properties present, which can also cause soft and hard spots. The softer will wear away more rapidly leaving an irregular surface rather like the skin on an orange. This is termed 'undercutting' or is sometimes referred to as more graphically 'orange peel'.

Water supply

It is possible to sand a gemstone without water and before the introduction of waterproof backing material most sanding was

Fig 9 Metal drum sander.

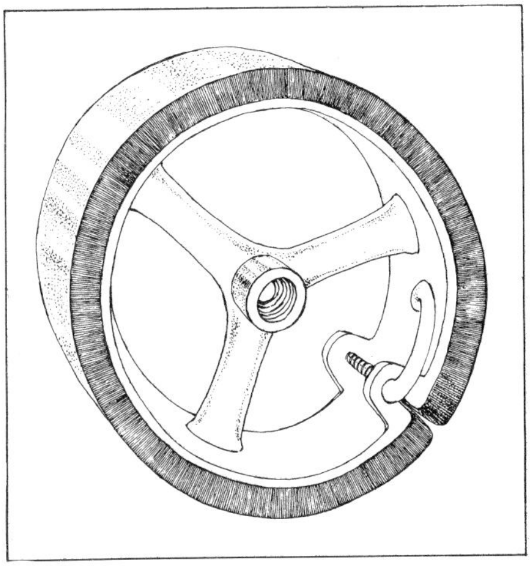

Fig 10 Arrangement for belt sander.

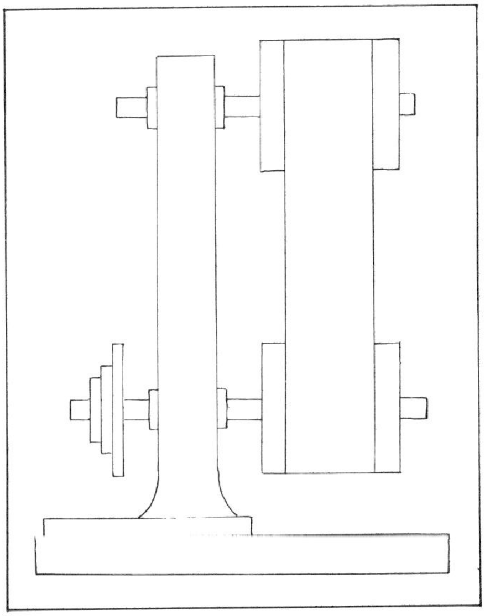

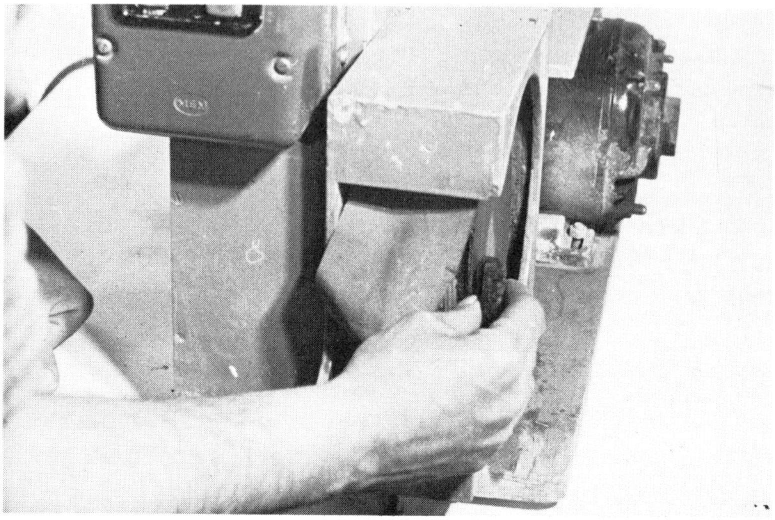

Plate 22 Using open fronted splash-hood for sanding.

done dry. Great care had to be taken, the main hazard being frictional heat, since overheating can cause the stone to crack or the dopping wax to melt so that the stone moves or drops off. Wet sanding eliminates these possibilities and also prevents the abrasive from clogging with stone dust. Most lapidaries sand wet as, apart from the advantages mentioned, a superior finish is obtainable because the depth of cut can be governed by regulating the amount of water. The water acts as a lubricant—more water gives less abrasion and less water means greater contact with the stone and a more rapid cut.

Wooden wheels and leather discs are better used on a vertical shaft, as the grit will stay in place longer. A mixture of water and grit can be applied from a squeezy bottle, the coarser grits having to be shaken before every application as they soon settle. All horizontal discs can be supplied with water by a regulated drip onto the centre, and centrifugal force will spread it to the edges.

Vertical discs need a fine jet of water directed at the centre. This can be supplied from a can, standing on a shelf above the machine, which has a rubber or plastic tube with a fine nozzle fitted to the end—the nozzle from a car windscreen washer is ideal.

Drum and belt sanders need two or three drips to cover the whole face. One method that can be used on all types of sanders is a plastic squeezy bottle. The hole in the top is usually far too big, but if the cap is left on, a very small hole can be drilled in it to give a fine jet.

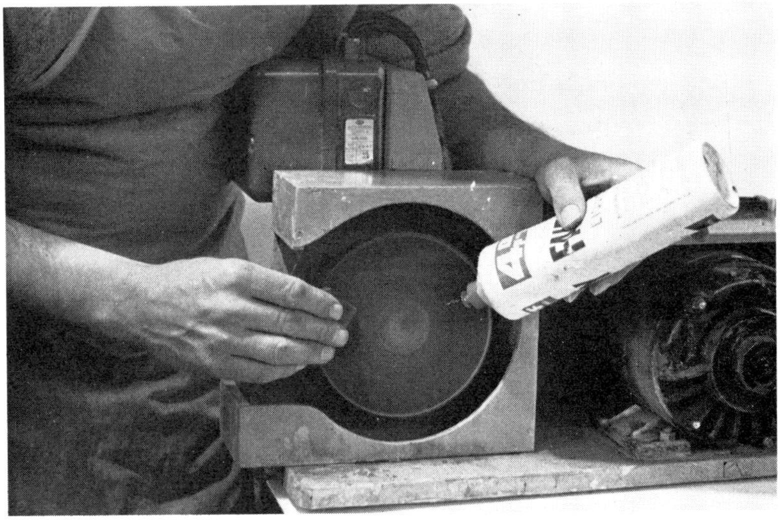

Plate 23 Standing position when using squeezy bottle.

A splash hood or ring should be provided to trap spray and grit which is then drained through a tube into a container: remember to empty this can on a piece of waste ground and not down the drain. On disc sanders it is useful to have enough room for the hand to be used in line with, or even slightly behind the disc, when the stone is held in the hand; this is shown in Plate 22.

Correct use of sander

A new sanding cloth cuts very much faster than when it is worn in; for this reason always try to sand harder stones on a new disc. The beginner should find out exactly how quickly a new disc cuts by pressing a small piece of agate firmly onto it.

When a curved surface has been ground allow it to dry completely before sanding, since on a wet stone these scratches are more difficult to see as they fill with water. For this reason, when examining at any stage of sanding, the stone must be perfectly dry.

Place a 220 grit cloth on the machine, switch on and take up the position shown in Plate 23.

This is a useful position to stand, especially if using a squeezy bottle to supply water. The left hand can rest on the top of the machine to direct the water and the operator is out of line of the spray.

Hold the stone firmly with the thumb one side and fingers the other and press it against the disc. With practice the pressure can be increased, so speeding up the sanding. The stone must be kept continuously on the move otherwise small flats are ground on the surface, and the whole point of coarse sanding is to remove the flats and scratches left by the grinding wheel. Final minor adjustments to the shape of the curve are made on this coarse cloth as the medium and fine cloths will not remove sufficient material to make any difference. Rotate the stone along its vertical axis and at the same time gradually alter the angle the horizontal axis offers to the sanding disc, thus completely sanding one half. Dry the stone and examine it carefully to note the difference between grinding marks and 220 sanding scratches; then complete the other half. On checking, all the scratches should be running in the same direction, any that are not are probably grinding marks and must be removed. Rotate the stone through 90 degrees and repeat until once again the scratches are all running in one direction.

Sometimes it is impossible to sand a small spot in the centre of the curve—this is usually the result of not making absolutely certain that the curve has been ground right to the centre on the grinding wheel. The quickest way to correct this is to re-grind and re-sand.

When satisfied, change to a medium cloth (320 grit) and repeat as for 220 sanding remembering to sand one half and compare 220 and 320 scratches.

The final sanding for most stones can be done with 400 or 500 grit, although very occasionally a 600 grit will be needed. Examine the stone carefully with a 10 magnification hand lens and even when the surface appears to be perfectly uniform time can be well spent in sanding for another 3 or 4 minutes; after a fair amount of experience a lapidary can very quickly decide which grit has caused a particular scratch.

The final quality of the polish on the gemstone depends on how well the sanding has been done. One mark left on the surface will spoil an otherwise perfect finish. Since coarser scratches cannot be removed on the polisher, the only way of erasing them is to go back to the sanding machine and start again. This obviously wastes time and is frustrating, so it is a much better policy to search really hard for marks when examining the stone rather than looking and hoping there are none.

5. POLISHING

The actual polishing of a gemstone is the final aim of the lapidary. The brilliant, mirror-like finish depends entirely on how well the previous stages have been completed, and much emphasis has already been placed on aiming for perfection when grinding and sanding. The lustre is produced by pressing the gemstone hard against softer materials such as felt, leather or wood, charged with a little polishing powder mixed with water.

There are two theories held as to how the shine is imparted to a gemstone. The first is that the polish is a form of very fine abrasive which produces scratches that are too small to be visible. The second, that atom size particles projecting above the surface are 'melted' partly by the chemical action of the agent and partly by heat caused through friction. This molten matter is spread to form a perfect surface flow which is known as the 'Beilby layer', and is rather like icing spread on a cake with a hot wet knife.

Many people prefer the former theory, but it must be remembered that a number of polishing agents are softer than the stones they are polishing. Also, most gemstones show a quite remarkable difference between a sanded and a polished surface. Irrespective of which theory is correct, it is the preparation of the surface which remains the most important fact.

Polishes

Different stones respond to different polishes, therefore a quantity of the following should be kept in stock:

Cerium oxide. Probably the best known and most widely used of the polishing agents, it is a pinkish powder which is comparatively cheap and is excellent for polishing most gemstones except those likely to undercut.

Tin oxide. A white powder that can usually be bought a little cheaper than cerium oxide, it is useful on leather for gems that undercut, and is the preferred polish for tumbling.

Chrome oxide. A green powder, quite useful for polishing jade, lapis lazuli and other undercutting stones, it is extremely messy to use as it stains hands and clothes green and is very difficult to remove.

Linde A. This, the most carefully graded of the aluminium oxides, is probably the best all-round polish. It is excellent for undercutting stones when used with wood or leather, but is very much more expensive than the others. A small quantity ought to be kept for the very special or difficult stone.

Each polish should be kept in its own container, which should be dustproof and clearly labelled. When not in use it should be stored in a cupboard well away from grinding and sanding apparatus.

Polishing buffs

The polishing buff is the vehicle for carrying the polish. Many different materials such as cork, carpet and cloth have been successfully used, but the three main ones are felt, leather and wood. One other material kept exclusively for polishing serpentine is corduroy which, used with crocus powder as the polish, gives an excellent finish.

Felt buffs

Felt is the most common material, and used with cerium oxide will polish a great variety of stones. The best quality felt is termed 'rock hard' and this should be specified when ordering, as others are much softer and will wear too rapidly. A good felt although expensive, will give many years of continuous use if it is not abused. Felt less than ¼in thick is rarely used as it will tend to wrinkle unless it is carefully glued down. If the edge of the felt wheel is going to be used, the material should be at least 1½in thick. Most polishing machines however, are designed to use the side of the wheel, which makes it easier to apply the polish and gives a larger area to work on.

Leather buffs

Leather buffs can be used for polishing almost any gemstone and their greatest use is in polishing materials that undercut. It has a very much slower polishing action than felt and as it polishes best when nearly dry, the stone heats up very quickly. The discs used are similar to those for sanding; a plywood or metal wheel with a soft rubber backing, but with a disc of thin leather in place of the sander. It is useful to have a leather disc fastened onto a slightly curved wooden wheel, as shown in Plate 24 for polishing flat surfaces. The leather should be soaked in water to make if soft and pliable, stretched over the surface, and then tacked in position.

Wooden buffs

Wooden buffs have been used for many years by professional

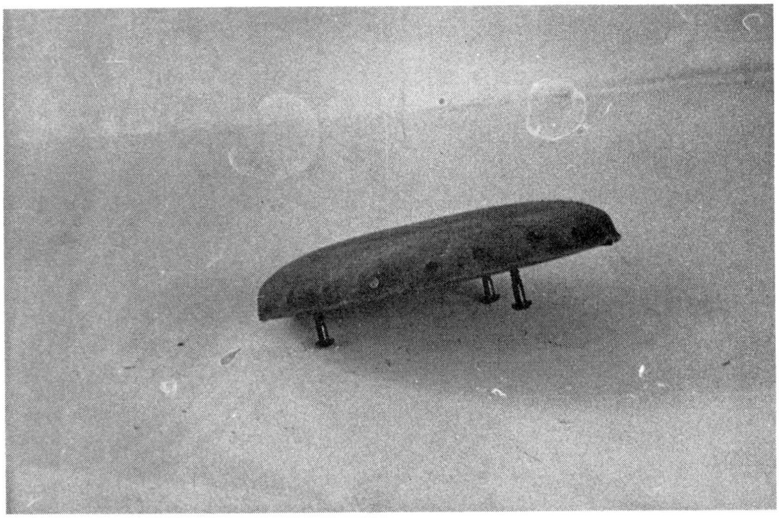

Plate 24 Sheet of leather fastened to curved wooden wheel.

lapidaries. Discs, drums, or wheels turned on a lathe are either left flat or have a variety of shaped grooves cut into the side or the edge; similar in action to leather, they are ideal for polishing undercutting and very hard stones. It is best to choose quarter sawn hardwood for these buffs as timber cut in this manner is less likely to warp. Soaking in hot paraffin wax will help to prevent water absorption.

Cleanliness is absolutely essential for polishing, as contamination of the buffs by foreign particles can not only scratch the stones but may ruin the buff. Each buff should be kept in its own self-sealing plastic container when not in use, clearly labelled and stored with the polishes well away from grits.

The beginner should start by buying a felt buff and then gradually build up a good selection. The following is a suggested list that should cover all needs: one flat felt, one curved felt made up in the same way as the curved leather, three soft backed leather, and three curved leather for use each with Linde A, tin and chrome oxide. Peel-em-off adhesive can be used on the soft-backed discs, but leather will tend to wrinkle so one of the contact adhesives is preferred.

Machinery

Polishing can be done successfully on a combination machine by replacing the sanding disc with a buff, but a separate polishing machine has much to commend it since a combination machine must be thoroughly cleaned down before use to make sure no particles of grit can contaminate the buff.

Plate 25 Home-built polisher using cheaper bearings.

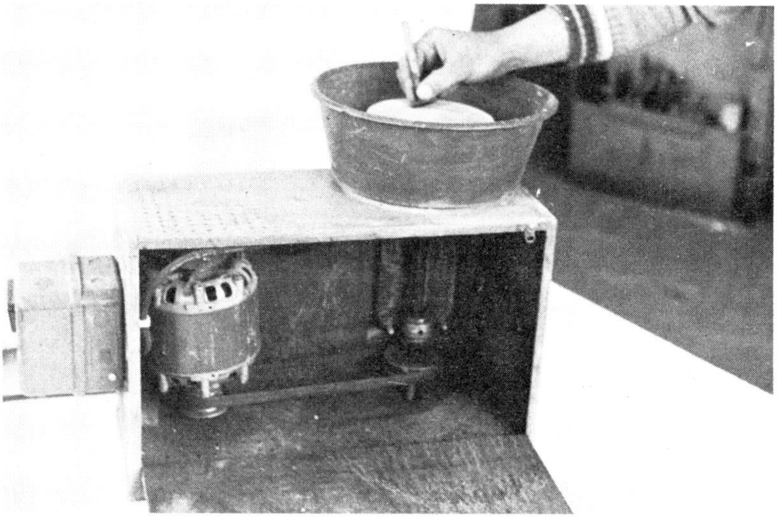

A separate polisher is fairly simple to make, and with very little water used, a sealed pan is not essential, so a plastic bowl as shown in Plate 25 is ideal.

Abrasive grits are not used, therefore sealed-for-life bearings are not essential and the very much cheaper plummer blocks with graphite impregnated bushes can be used.

Buffs mounted on a vertical shaft have several advantages—the polish is easier to apply to the centre, and it is easier to polish larger stones that require holding in both hands.

Low speed is essential for the polishing operation. It is the only stage where insufficient water is used to keep the stone cool, and high speeds would very quickly result in overheating. As even at low speed an amount of polish is thrown off and wasted, high speed would give a much higher rate of wastage. Speeds of between 400 and 800 r.p.m. for a 6in buff are acceptable.

Polishing

When sanding is finished it is important to wash thoroughly the stone, hands, and in particular the finger nails *before* setting up for polishing. If the gemstone is mounted on a dop stick, make sure the wax is washed and pay particular attention to the edges of slices that are left with their original rough edge, as seen in some of the colour plates. An old toothbrush makes an excellent miniature scrubbing brush.

Select the right combination of buff and polish for the stone being used and place the buff on the machine. The correct combination for most common stones can be found in

Chapter 10, but never assume that the given combination is always the correct one for every piece of stone of that type. Whenever a finish is less than satisfactory, and the sanding has been done properly, experiment with different combinations.

Mix the polishing agent in a glass or plastic container in the proportion of approximately one part polish to ten of water by volume. Add two or three drops of detergent to act as a wetting agent; this allows the water to soak more rapidly and to help the polish to be more evenly distributed. If the container has a dust-tight lid the polish can be stored indefinitely and is always ready for use providing it is kept covered with water.

Each container should be clearly labelled and have its own brush; brushes having no metal parts are best as they can be left in the container without rusting—once again toothbrushes are useful. The mixture is applied by dipping the brush into the thinner mix at the top of the container and holding it against the spinning buff. The powder settles quite quickly and should be stirred well before each application, but do not use this thicker sludge from the bottom as this is not only wasteful, but can slow the polishing action.

If a new felt buff is being used, or one that has not been used for some time, wet it with plain water from a squeezy bottle before putting on the polish; if this is not done a great deal of polish will be wasted in just wetting the buff. A squeezy bottle can also be used for mixing and applying the polish, shaking it well to mix the powder and water thoroughly and then squeezing as much as is needed onto the buff. For a felt buff only enough of the mixture to colour it should be used, and more added every few minutes to keep the surface damp, but not wet. If the polish tends to build up on the buff use plain water to dampen it and add more water to the mixture.

A great deal of pressure is needed during polishing irrespective of the type of buff used. This pressure may vary from a few ounces to many pounds, depending on the size and type of stone being polished, the correct amount needed being judged accurately only with experience. The greater the pressure, however, the more heat is generated and great care is needed otherwise the stone could crack. Test the temperature of the stone by touching it against the back of the hand as this part is fairly sensitive; as soon as the stone becomes hot it must be left to cool. It is good practice to have several stones ready for polishing so that as soon as one begins to heat up it can be put down to cool whilst working on the next.

Plate 26 Correct position for holding stone for polishing. Note how the trailing edge of the stone is clear of the buff.

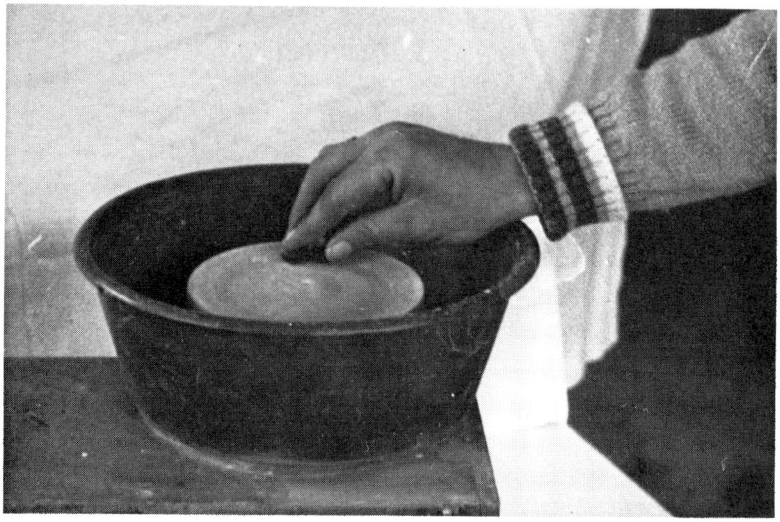

A systematic approach to polishing is useful to make sure that the whole surface is covered, and as the edges of the stone are usually slightly more difficult to do it is best to polish these first. Hold the stone so that the leading edge is clear of the buff so that it will not catch and be torn from the fingers. This is shown in Plate 26.

Work with a slight rolling action, from the centre of the buff to the edge and back again. This last point is important as if only one area is used a hollow will develop, though it can be flattened by holding a block of pumice stone against the spinning wheel: pumice stone can also be used to clean a contaminated surface.

Polish the edges of the stone until a perfect finish has been obtained around the circumference. Gradually lower the angle of incidence and work in concentric circles until the whole of the surface has been polished. A box or roll of disposable tissue is needed to wipe the surface frequently for careful examination as polishing powder can hide small unpolished patches or scratches. If scratches are noticed, don't waste time trying to polish them out, but return to the sander.

When the whole surface has been polished, wash the stone thoroughly, dry it and examine it critically under a strong light—any reflection from the surface should be mirror-like. Rotate the stone and check that the image of the light source moving slowly over the whole surface remains sharp and clear. If any dull patches are noticed, and scratches are not apparent, these areas may have been missed so try polishing them. Sometimes, particularly with the beginner, the surface appears to be rippled, which is probably an indication that there are small flat surfaces left from the 220 sanding disc caused through moving the stone too slowly. The only remedy here is to return to the 220 disc, remove the flats and re-sand on 320 and 400.

A really severe test is to examine a polished surface through a 10x eye glass — a perfectly polished surface is almost impossible to see. Any properly sanded gemstone should begin to show a polish within seconds; if it does not the wrong buff/polish combination is being used.

Felt will polish most common gemstones, but those that undercut will quickly develop pits and depressions which get deeper very rapidly. At the first signs of this happening, switch off and change to a wood or leather disc. If choosing leather, wet the surface of the disc with water to which a few drops of detergent have been added, to make it soft and pliable, then switch on and leave the machine to run for a minute so that surplus water is thrown off. Apply a very small quantity of chrome oxide or Linde A and work the stone from the centre to the edge of the disc in the same way as for felt.

To begin with the leather will be too wet and the stone will slide, but as the surface dries out a strong tugging will be felt and it is in this state that the best polishing takes place. This state of near dryness must be maintained by applying only a few drops of water, and these near the centre. Overheating is an even greater problem when using leather buffs and a strict check must be kept on the stone to prevent it cracking.

6. COMBINATION MACHINES

It is advisable when setting up for lapidary to remember that a great deal of money can be spent, and if the hobby does not hold your interest it can mean money wasted. Against this is the gratifying fact that very few second-hand machines are offered for sale—inferring that most novices graduate to devotees.

Joining a club or society, talking to other lapidaries and if possible trying various machines, can be helpful in making the decision as to which type of machine to buy. Although the ideal set-up is to have a separate machine for each process, this is not always possible.

Most beginners usually decide on a combination machine which, as its name suggests, is capable of a variety of operations. These range from an inexpensive machine with a single, short shaft with interchangeable accessories, to a larger and more sophisticated arrangement. The main disadvantage of the former is that parts have to be changed for each operation and care has to be taken when replacing the grinding wheel to make sure it is balanced. The other system usually means that once a grinding wheel has been fixed it remains on the shaft until it is renewed.

Plate 27 Highland Park 8in combination unit.

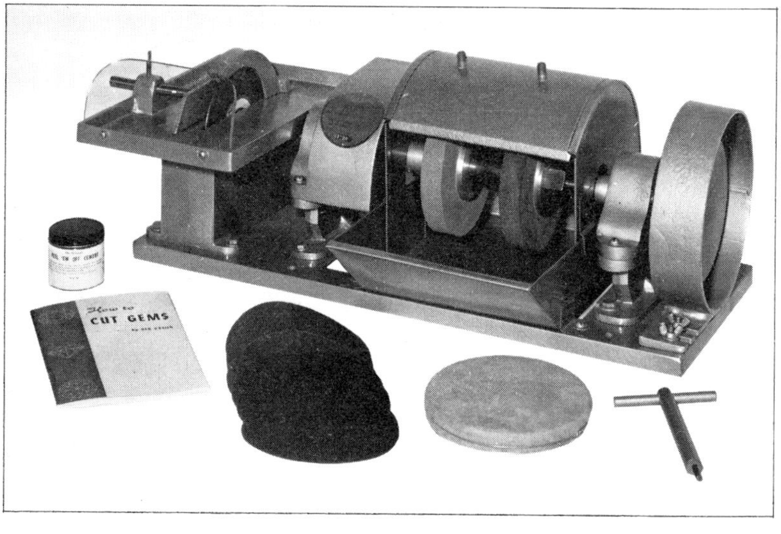

Opposite: Tiger eye (top) and banded agate (bottom).

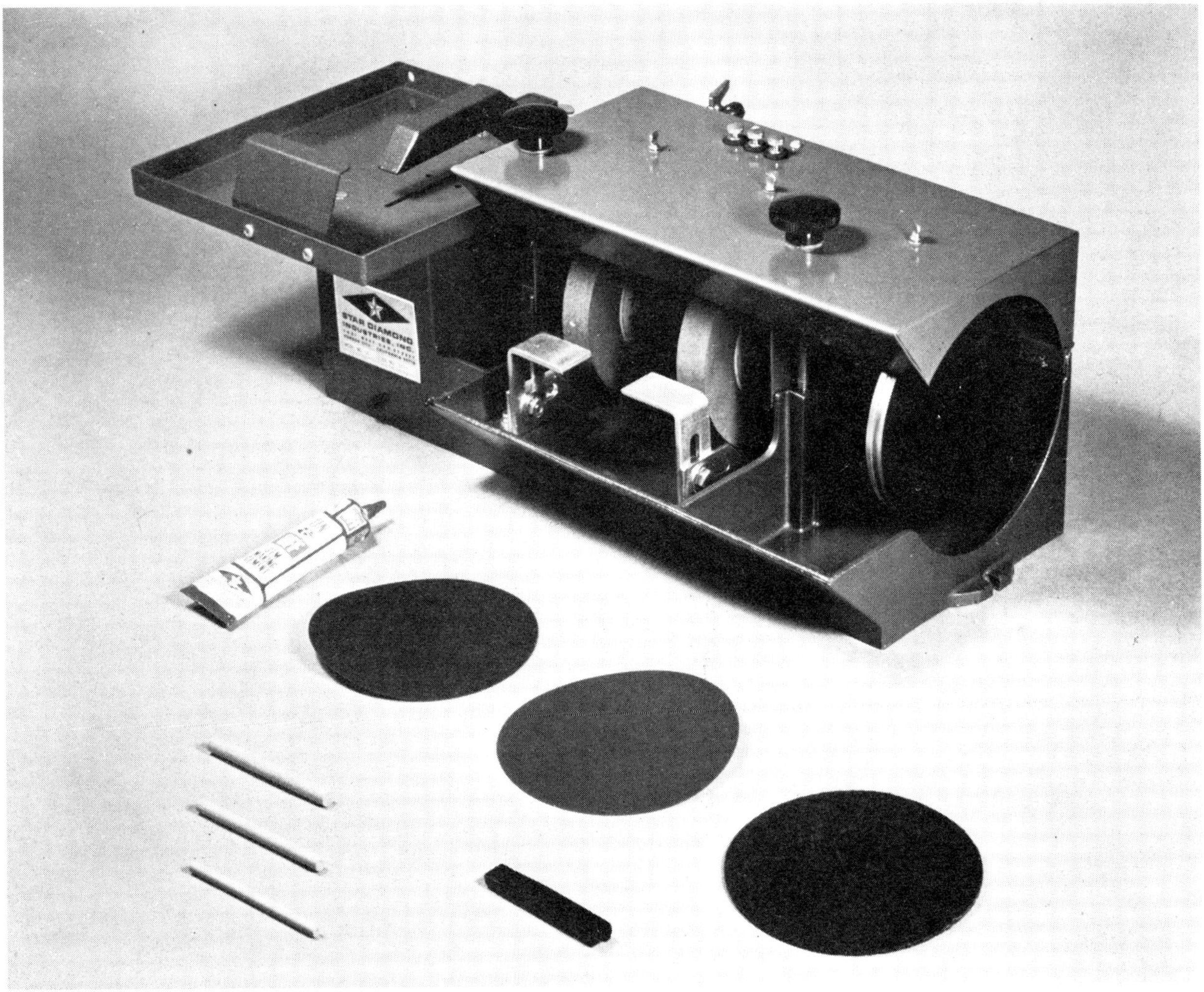

Plate 28 Star Diamond Cab Workshop 6in combination unit.

Separate machines take up more space and need separate motors, switches and wiring, but they are designed for the best possible performance, while combination machines have to have many compromises, particularly in relation to ideal speeds—the saw, for example, is turning throughout all other operations and, unless the tank is drained, is constantly spraying oil. Most combinations have a 6in saw blade, which is limited in its use, and as two people will find they can work at the same time, extra safety precautions have to be observed.

The main advantages of combination machines are that they can be portable, which is necessary if the bench is normally used for other work—they can easily be stored away when not in use; that they are very compact, which is important if space is

Opposite: Brazilian agates (left and bottom right) and moss agates (top right).

Plate 29 Whithear 8in combination machine, made up of three separate units connected together by shaft couplings.

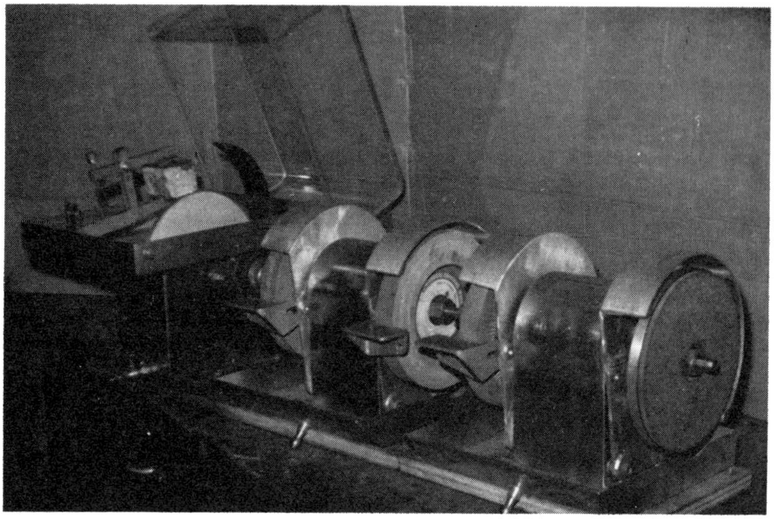

Plate 30 Gemtek 6in combination unit. The cast aluminium machine parts and various accessories can be purchased separately for building this machine.

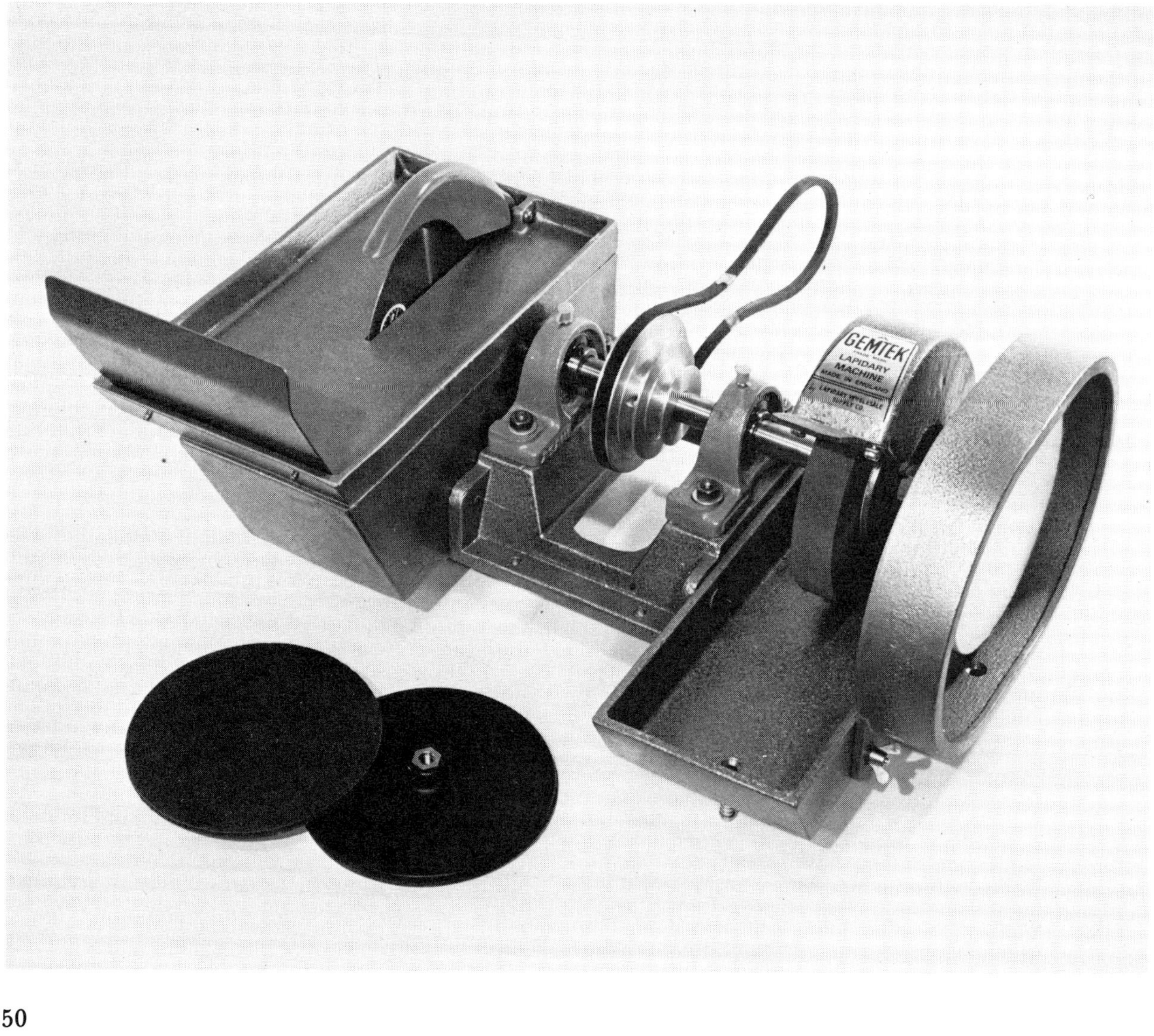

very limited; and that they are very much cheaper than separate machines.

One possibility is a compromise between separate and combination machines—a separate saw, as large as possible; a combined grinder/sander; and a combined lap and polishing machine.

There are two main types of combination machine: those with the wheels mounted vertically [Plates 27-33] and those mounted horizontally [Plates 34-36].

Horizontal shaft combinations

These are probably the most common and offer a great number of combinations—saw/grinder, grinder/sander, grinder/

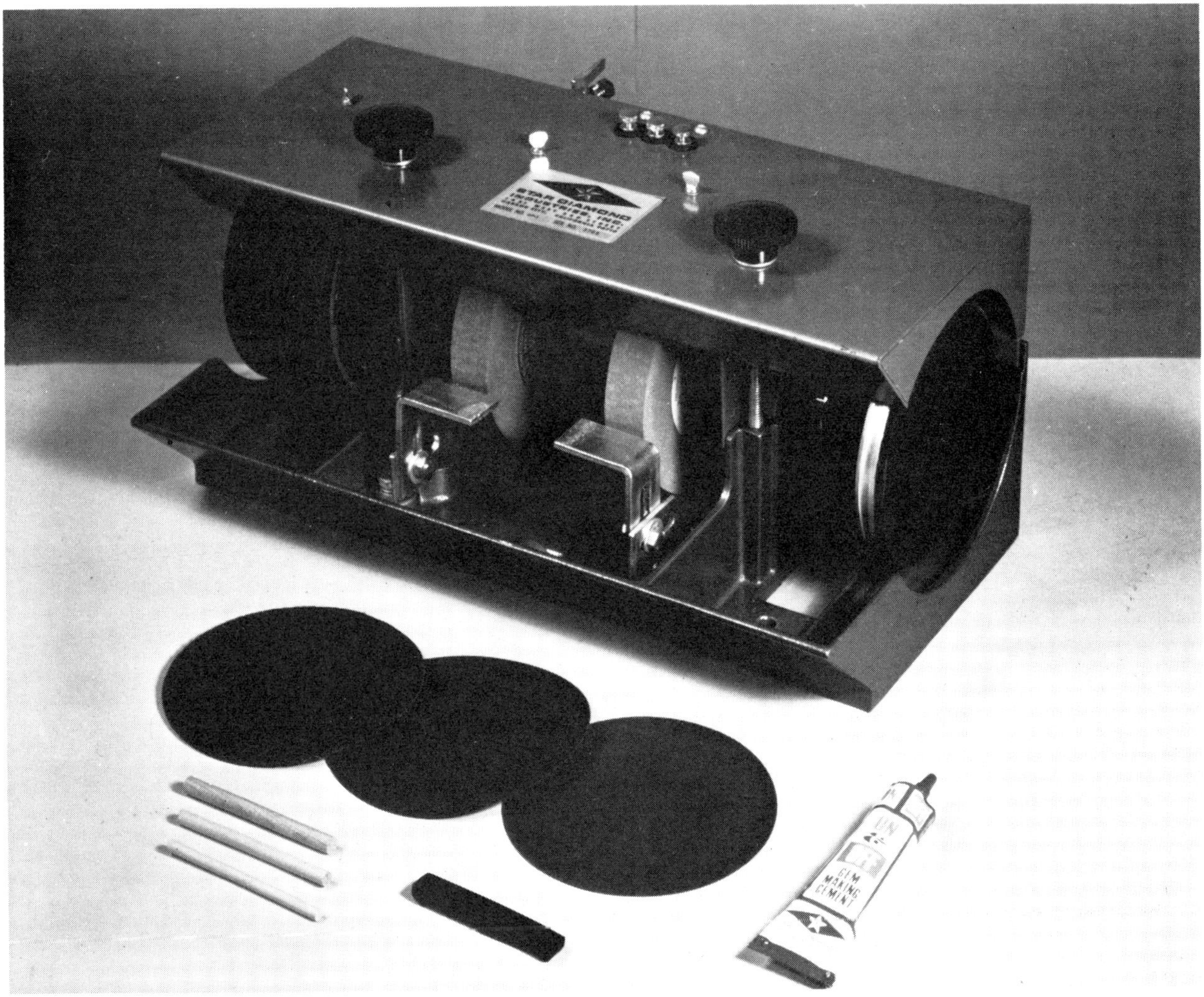

Plate 31 Star Diamond 6in grinder-polisher.

sander/polisher, or the complete saw/grinder/sander/polisher. They are basically designed for cabochon work, and the usual set-up is one long shaft with the saw at one end, grinding wheel or wheels in the centre, with a disc/sander/polisher at the other end. The operator can start with the saw and work through the various processes needing only to change discs for sanding and polishing. The motor is usually mounted behind the shaft out of the way, and a vee belt connects it to a three-stage pulley in the centre of the shaft. When the grinding wheels need replacing it usually means unbolting various parts of the machine, which affords an opportunity for a thorough clean.

Vertical shaft combinations

These are almost as popular and consist of a single, vertical, threaded shaft passing through a splash pan; the top of the

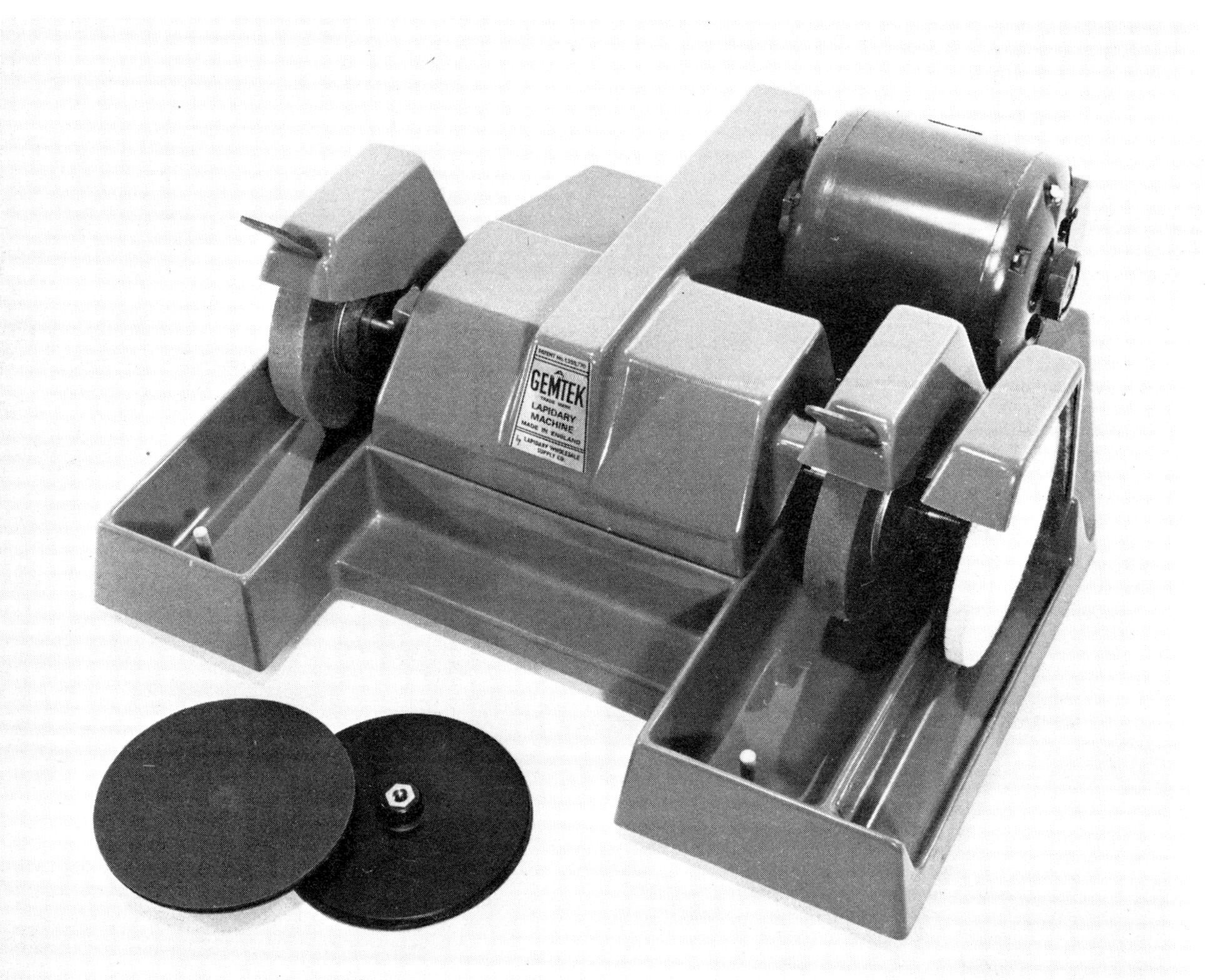

Plate 32 Gemtek 6in double grinder-sander-polisher.

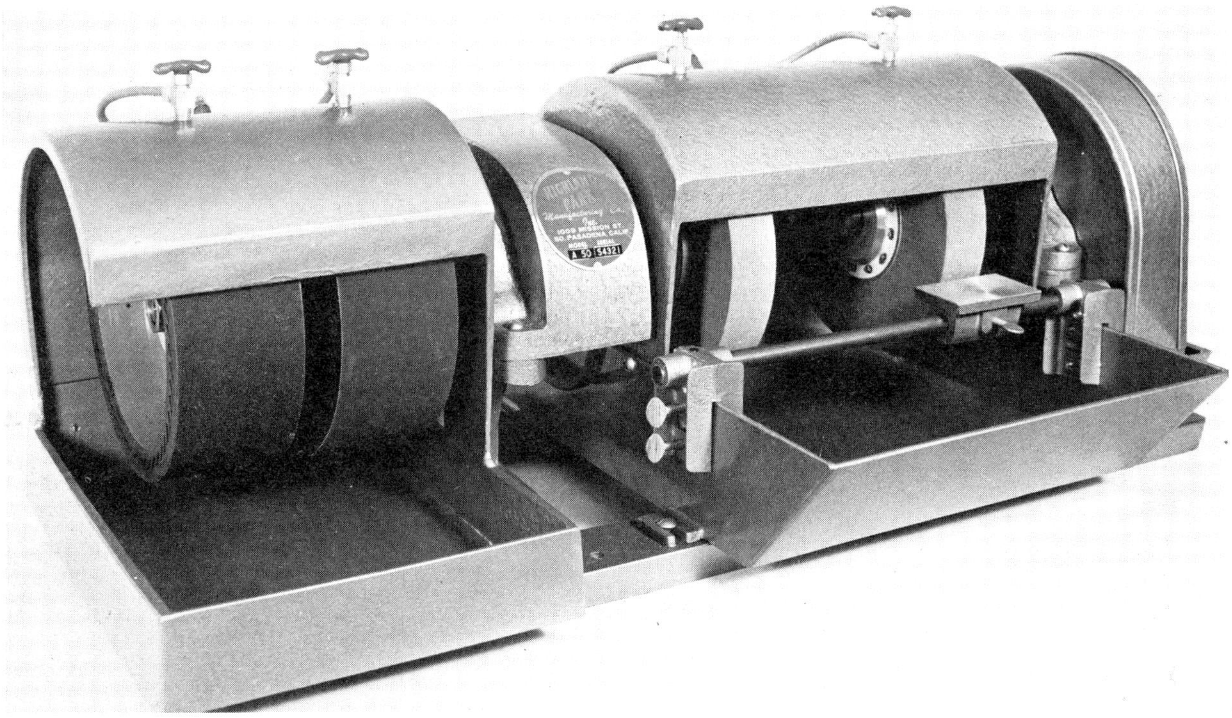

Plate 33 Highland Park 8CD 8in grinding, sanding and polishing unit.

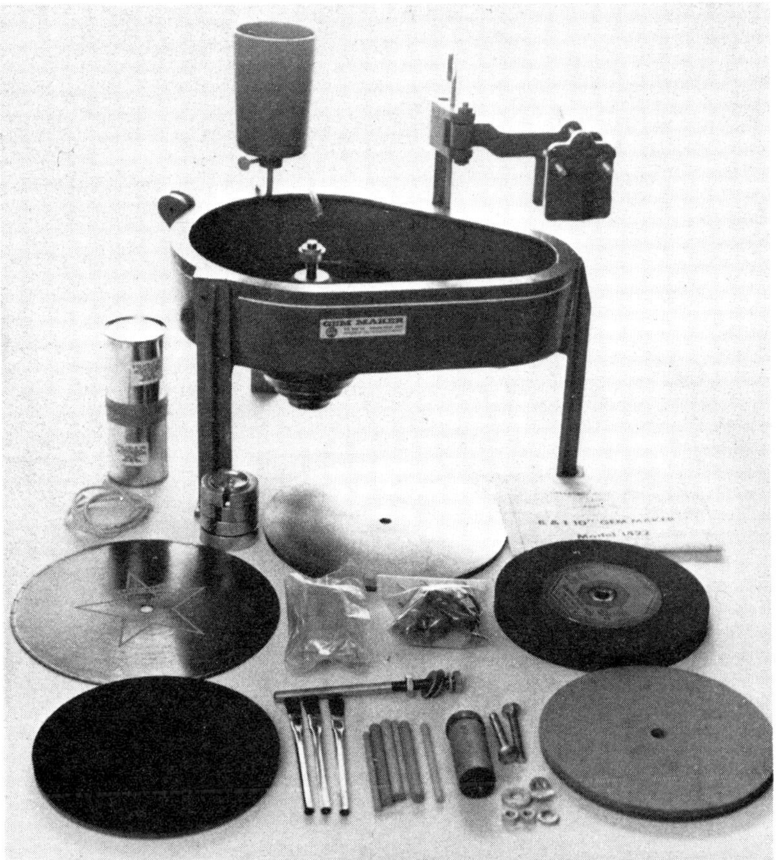

Plate 34 B & I 10in combination machine

shaft is stepped down to form a shoulder for a flange to rest on Some accessories are threaded on to the shaft, while others are slipped over and held in place by a locking nut.

The great versatility of this type of machine is the number of accessories available for the one shaft. Apart from the usual saw, grinding wheel, sanding discs and polishing buff, there is available a steel lap for flat lapping, and a faceting head for use with loose grit or diamond-impregnated copper discs; the advantages and disadvantages of this type of machine for grinding have already been mentioned in Chapter 3. Sawing, particularly trim sawing, is perhaps not quite so easy on a vertical shaft machine, but with all its accessories it can be a complete lapidary workshop. Another advantage is that the

Plate 35 Robilt 6in combination machine with some of its accessories.

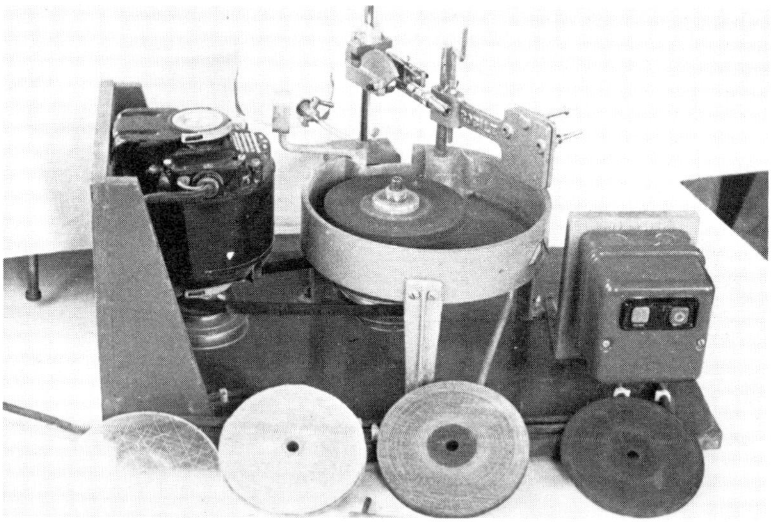

Plate 36 Gem Master combination machine.

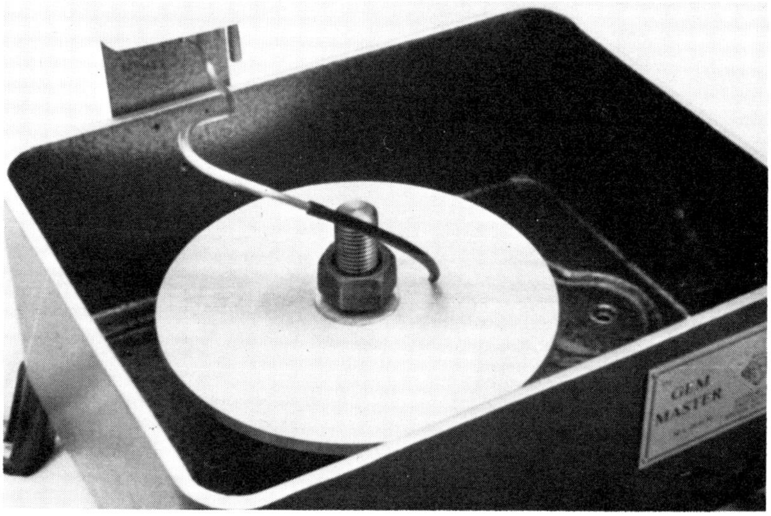

basic machine can be purchased relatively cheaply and other accessories added when the need arises.

Home built combinations

Basic construction kits are available from some suppliers, which will cut down on the initial costs. Most good machine-tool shops stock a large variety of suitable shafts, bearings, pulleys, and belts for building from scratch, and if this is the intention, the earlier suggestion of having three machines including a separate saw, is probably the best solution. The great advantage of home built machinery is that it can be tailor-made to suit personal requirements.

All machines need to be mounted. If they are to be portable, a solid baseboard is required, preferably with rubber feet to prevent it sliding on the bench, and if space permits it is best to build a special, sturdy stand with cupboards underneath for storing accessories such as discs and grits.

7. LAPPING

Lapping is the process of grinding a rough surface flat and smooth, by holding the rock face against the face of the lap—a flat plate of mild steel or cast iron—with the contact surfaces charged with abrasive grit.

Initially, one uses coarse grit, to flatten the surface as quickly as possible, progressively changing to finer grits until the overall result is a very delicate 'frosting' effect; the finest grits of all will render this virtually invisible, leaving just a matt surface.

Lapping works on the principle that the particles of abrasive chip tiny pits into the rock surface; the finer the grit, the more microscopic the pits. The more accurate a surface can be cut on the saw, the less work there is on the lapping tool—but even small saw scratches on a large surface, usually caused by cutting too quickly, mean that the whole face has to be taken down to the bottom of the deepest hollow.

Lapping of small surfaces can be done on the side of a grinding wheel, but this will very quickly wear a concave depression in the grinder, making it no longer true.

Laps must be mounted on a vertical shaft, otherwise the grit will drop off. A suggested layout is shown in figure 12.

Fig 11 Loose grit chipping out small pieces of rock.

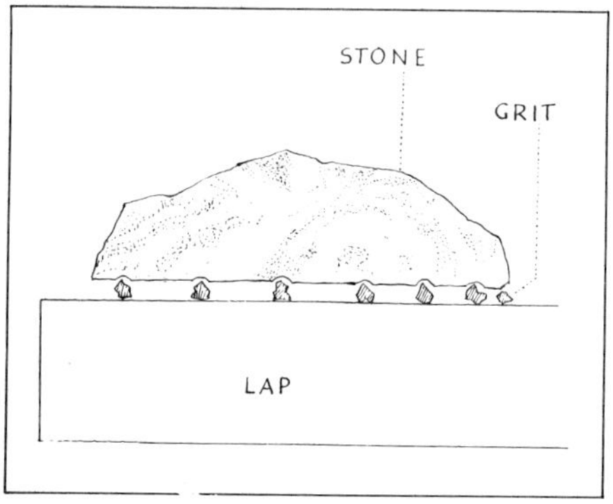

In a thick plywood box, a sealed-for-life bearing is bolted to the underside of the top, and a thrust bearing is bolted to the bottom; a pulley is mounted on the shaft between them [Plate 37]. The pulley needs to be large to bring the speed right down to between 300 and 400 r.p.m. otherwise too much grit will be thrown off.

The splash pan should be removable for easy cleaning; a large plastic bowl is ideal for this, particularly if ribbed on the bottom, since these ribs will prevent water reaching the centre of the bowl and running down the shaft. Failing this, a ring of wood can be mounted underneath the centre of the bowl to force it higher. Commercial machines are available; such a machine is shown in Plate 38.

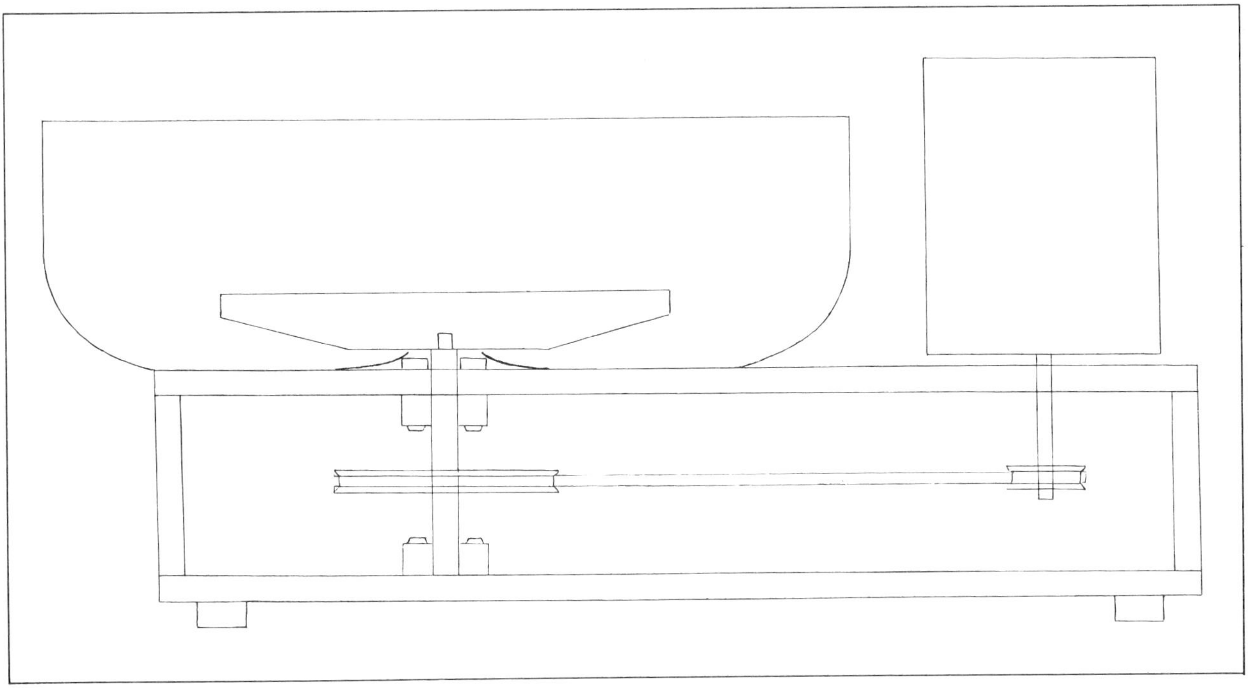

Fig 12 Suggested construction for a lapping machine.

Lapping grits

Silicon carbide loose grit bought by weight is the abrasive used and must be carefully stored to avoid cross-contamination. Larger or badly sawn pieces of rock need a grit as coarse as 60, while smaller, flatter pieces can be ground flat using 220 grit. Fine lapping is done with 500 or 600 grit, or even finer if it can be obtained; the finer the grit the more expensive it is, but very little is needed.

Loose grits are usually sold in plastic bags and need to be transferred to a sturdier container as soon as possible, and carefully labelled and stored. Wide topped plastic containers with a lid, about 3 to 4ins tall and the same diameter, are ideal for mixing water with the grit. There must be one box for each grade of grit, and each with its own brush. Ideally a brush without metal parts is best so that it can be stored inside its container with no risk of corrosion; thus a full-bristled toothbrush, bent at the neck by softening the plastic, is perfect for the job.

Some lapidaries use squeezy bottles as dispensers, shaking them well before each application, but these tend to give too wet a mix, and fail to distribute the paste as evenly as a brush would.

Another essential when lapping is a deep bucket filled with water to which detergent has been added, for washing hands

Plate 37 Home-built lapping and polishing machine.

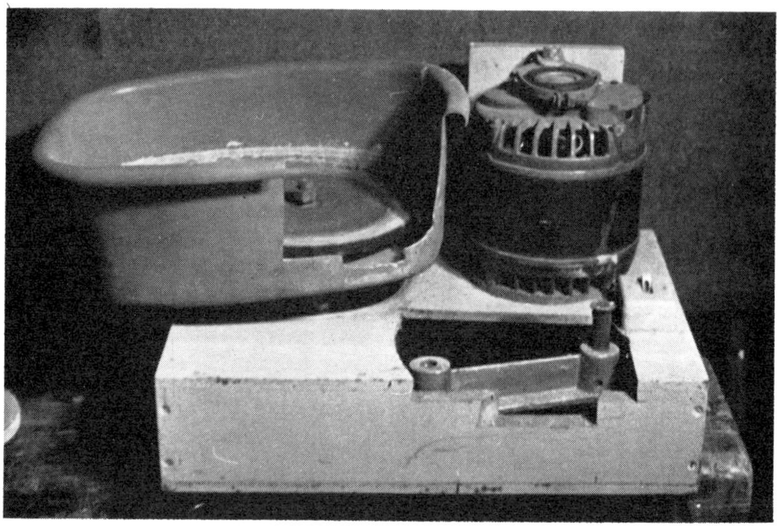

and the rock. Grits, being heavy, soon sink so there is little chance of picking up coarser grits when washing finer ones; the water discolouration is caused by extremely fine particles of abrasive and stone which are too small to scratch the rock.

Quite often lapidaries line the splash pan with sheets of newspaper, tucking them underneath the lap and over the sides of the pan and holding them in place with clothes pegs. If the newspaper is changed whenever one progresses to a finer grit size, then a stone which drops into the pan will come into contact only with the same size grit as is being used. Another precaution is to clean the pan thoroughly between each grit change, but as this is a lengthy job it is worth doing only if working on many stones at one stage. A compromise is to use the coarse grit without paper and then line the pan for future grades; as a great deal of the coarse grit is thrown off the lap into the pan, the brush can then be used to pick it up and put it back on the lap. The finer grits are not thrown off quite so readily.

Lapping

Pour about ½in of the coarse dry grit into the plastic container, cover with about the same amount of water, mix thoroughly and apply a brushful close to the centre of the rotating lap. Place the stone on top of the grit and, with just enough pressure to hold it, move it to the edge to distribute the grit; a very harsh, 'gritty' sound denotes that the grinding has begun.

If the stone is large enough, hold it with both hands and move it slowly across the entire face of the lap, going very slowly across the centre, where the lap itself is motionless. Keep the pressure

Opposite: Plate 38 Gemtek 6in lapping and polishing machine.

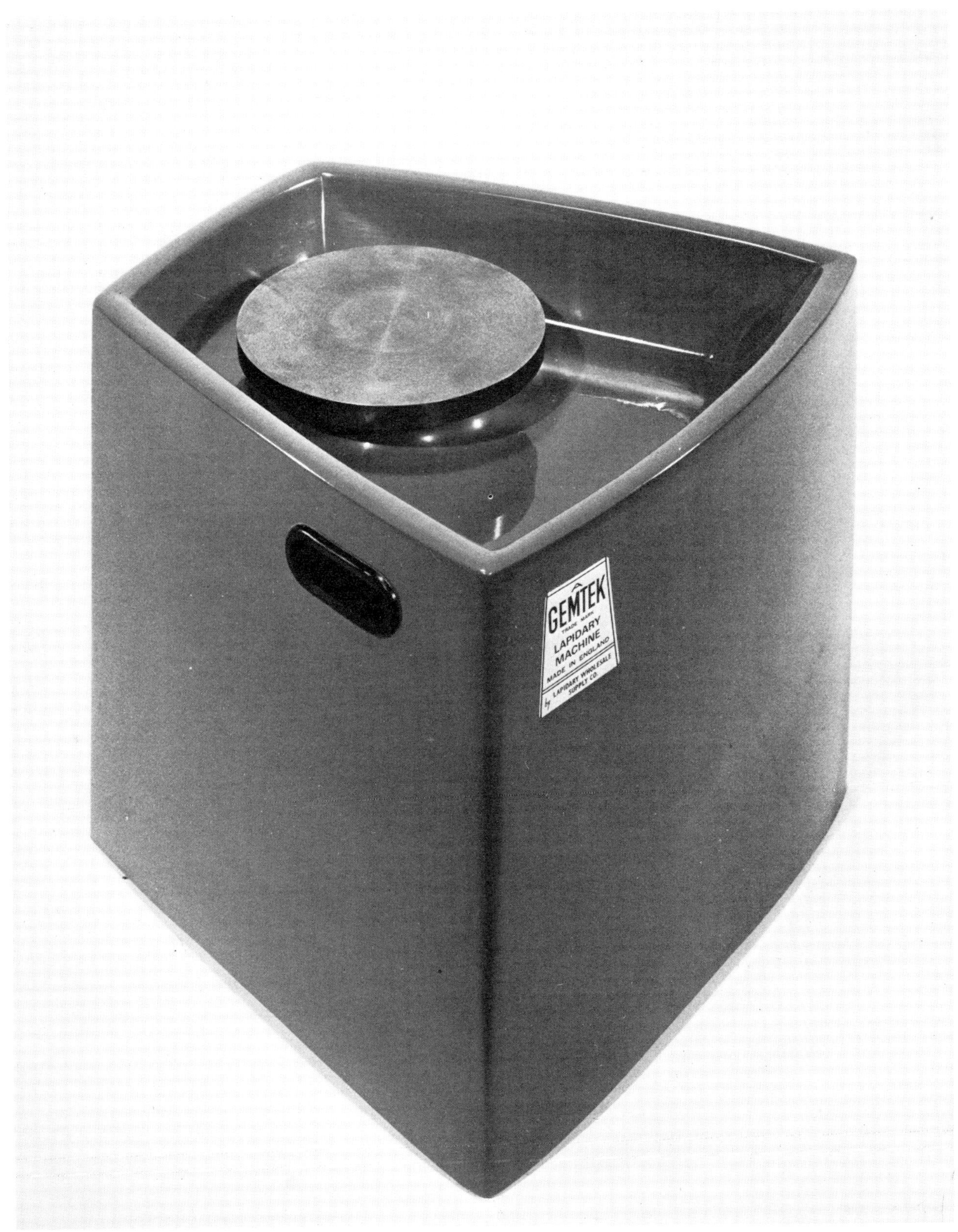
GEMTEK
TRADE MARK
LAPIDARY
MACHINE
MADE IN ENGLAND
by LAPIDARY WHOLESALE
SUPPLY CO.

very light, to avoid the grit being crushed unduly early, and keep the pressure even, since any imbalance will result in a convex surface on the stone.

After every two or three sweeps across the lap, rotate the stone's working face through 90 degrees to present a new leading edge, and remember to work to the very edge of the lap, since in time it could wear out of true.

It is important to get the right amount of water on the lap: one should aim for sufficient to form a slurry; too much and the grit is thrown off very quickly; too little and the lap dries off too quickly which can cause quite a violent 'snatching'. A large stone thrown off, even at this low speed, can easily be damaged.

After about 30 to 40 seconds the harsh sound will reduce to more of a 'swishing' sound, which means the grit has either been crushed or thrown off and another brushful must be applied.

It is impossible to give even a rough estimate of time needed for lapping as so many factors have to be taken into account, the main ones being the hardness and size of the rock and the accuracy of the surface at the outset.

When the face appears to be flat, wash the stone and dry it thoroughly; the frosty appearance will not show until the water has dried out of the tiny pits. Now examine the surface carefully by rotating it so that light strikes it from all angles; the surface should be completely frosted. Any low spots that have not been touched will show up fairly easily on most rocks as the texture will be different, usually showing a slight lustre. Coarse lapping must be continued until the surface is completely uniform, and even when this stage has been reached it is better to lap for a few more minutes.

When the coarse work is finished, place the brush in its container, put the lid on, wipe the outside and put the pot away. The lap must also be well washed, using plenty of soapy water and running the finger from centre to edge of the rotating disc to feel for any particles left: it only takes one piece of coarse grit on the lap to leave scratches on the next operation. Wash the stone and hands well, paying particular attention to finger nails and rough edges on the stone, since it is imperative to make sure all coarser grit is removed before starting with a finer.

Now would be the time to line the pan with newspaper, before mixing and applying the next grit and working in the same way as before. Many stones can now be fine lapped on 500 grit but some, particularly banded agates, show a slight difference in density in some bands. These tend to form slightly deeper pits and need lapping on an intermediate grit of 220 or 320 mesh.

Fine lapping should remove the frosty appearance by leaving pits in the surface which are too small to be seen, but in this stage the amount of water used is even more critical. If the lap is slightly too wet or too dry the stone tends to stick and can be torn from the hands. Aim for a watery slurry, sometimes brushing water from the top of the mixture without mixing it. Pressure is the same as for coarse lapping, using just enough to keep the stone in contact with the disc.

Dry the rock surface thoroughly and examine it for any small patches of frostiness through a 10x eye glass; it should be free from any pits or scratches.

Very thin rock slices can be difficult to hold in the fingers at any stage of lapping. One way to overcome this is to lap and polish a cut face on a larger piece of rock, slicing it off as the last operation. If the sample is small enough it can be fastened to a dop stick as described in Chapter 8, or cemented onto a block of wood with dopping wax.

Hand lapping

This very simple form of lapping requires only three sheets of plate glass about 8in square, and 80, 220 and 500 grit. The method is not recommended for large pieces of hard rock that need a lot of material removed, as it is very, very slow, being ideal for lapping flat surfaces on small, very thin sections for use with doublets and triplets, as described in Chapter 8, though larger pieces of softer material such as calcite, serpentine and Connemara marble can be hand-lapped very successfully. The colour plates showing Landscape marble and Mull granite were lapped by hand, although the granite took quite a long time.

The actual process of lapping by hand is very simple: put three or four drops of water on to the centre of the glass and add just a pinch of 80 grit. Place the stone on the grit and, using very little pressure, move it anti-clockwise in circles of about 1in diameter, gradually working around the centre of the plate as shown in figure 13.

Fig 13 Path followed by the stone being hand lapped.

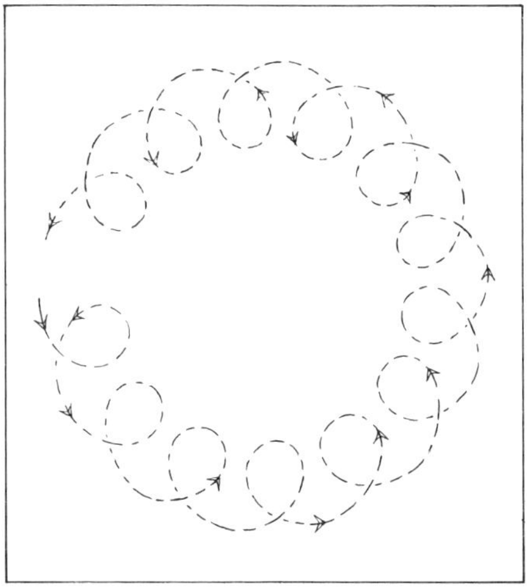

The grit will tend to move away from the centre and spill over the edge of the plate, which can be overcome to a certain extent by moving the hand, from the wrist, in an anti-clockwise direction and so rotating the stone through 90 degrees by every fourth or fifth completed sweep. Turning the stone in this manner will tend to push the grit into the centre. Continue the procedure for every grade of grit, washing the stone well, between operations.

Hand-polishing can be done on a piece of felt or leather glued to a slightly curved piece of wood; the stone will have to be pressed very hard onto the buff and rubbed quickly, to build up friction.

The following practise is not strictly lapping at all, but can be used in conjunction with it when perhaps a curved surface is required on a block that has been hand lapped on the edges.

The two pieces of serpentine shown facing page 17 were shaped and polished entirely by hand. The red piece needed very little shaping, but the green was cut from a fairly large block. Serpentine is one of the soft rocks—about 3 on Moh's hardness scale—which can be cut with a hacksaw, using slow, steady strokes and a coarse blade. The biggest problem was in finding some method of holding the rock steady, as both hands were needed to use the saw. The answer in this case proved to be epoxy resin: one side of the block was flat enough to be glued to a piece of wood, which was then cramped to the bench.

Another possibility would have been to set the rough rock in plaster of Paris; once the sides had been cut, the block could be cramped easily enough for the rest of the sawing.

The curves on the faces were achieved with a coarse file and the sanding done with the usual grades of wet or dry paper wrapped around a flat block of wood; sanding can be done dry, but the stone dust quickly clogs the paper. For slightly harder rocks an 80 or 100 grit paper can be introduced for the first sanding, and for more domed shapes it is better to dispense with the wood block and hold the paper in the hand.

Both pieces of serpentine were polished by rubbing crocus compound onto a piece of corduroy which was then rubbed hard onto the stone: other materials will respond better to the method described in hand lapping.

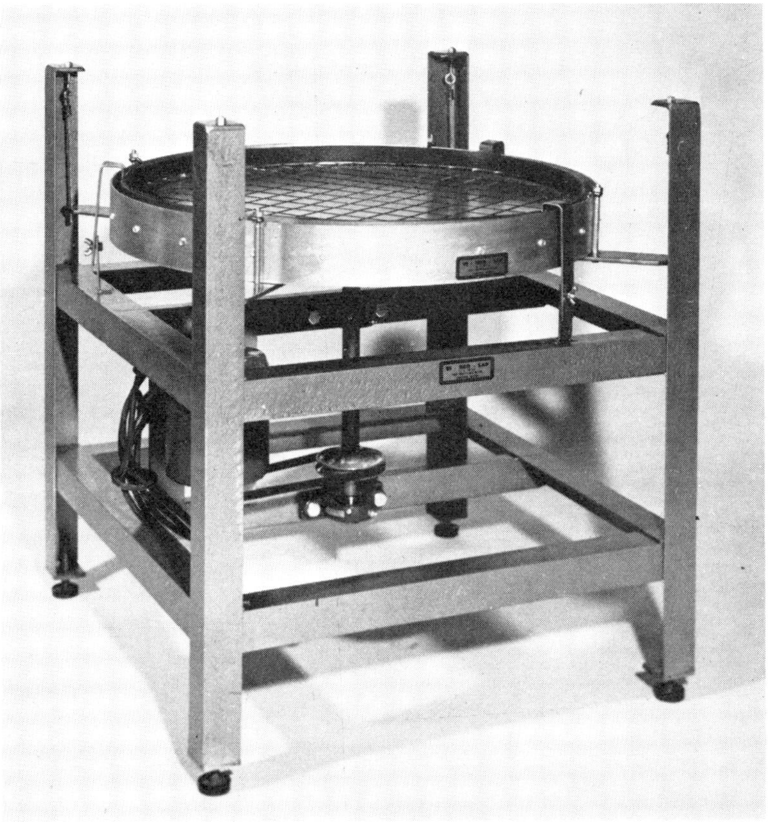

Plate 39 Highland Park 20in VI-Bro—Lap.

Automatic laps

Automatic laps take all the hard work and finger ache out of lapping—and all the sense of personal achievement. The only advantage of this type of machine comes when there are large numbers of specimens for working. An electric motor drives an eccentric shaft connected to the lap causing it to vibrate rapidly. The stones placed on the surface remain almost stationary whilst the water/grit mixture circulates under them in grooves cut into the surface of the lap. The order of working is the same as for normal lapping and each stage takes from 5 to 7 hours depending on hardness, size and accuracy of surface. Two different sizes of vibrating laps are shown in Plates 39 and 40.

Polishing

Polishing of all flat surfaces—as opposed to tiny flats on a faceted stone—is best done on a very slightly convex buff. Wooden wheels, curved leather as shown in Plate 24, or a felt buff made in the same way using ¼in thick felt instead of leather, are ideal. When polishing on a flat buff the surface 'gives' enough to make it easy to polish the edges but very difficult to reach the centre.

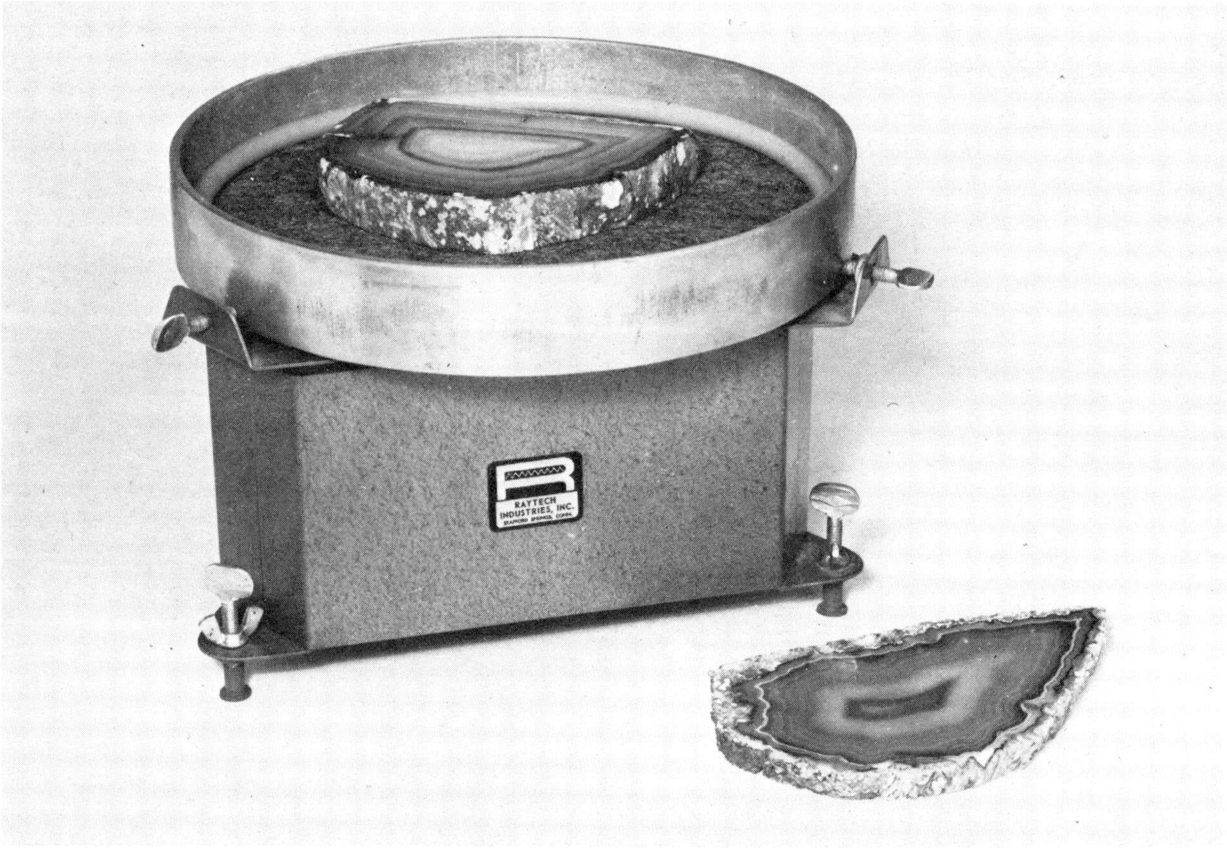

Plate 40 Raytech 10in vibrating lap.

Care must be taken when working on large samples, as it is possible to put on great pressure and heat the surface rapidly. On thin slices this heat is transmitted to the fingers very quickly and acts as a reminder, sometimes, however, coming too late when the stone has already cracked. Apart from checking on possible overheating when using cerium oxide on wood or felt, make sure it does not run too dry otherwise the polish can form into a hard particle and scratch the surface.

Opposite: Moroccan agate (top right) Brazilian agate (top left) Mexican coconut (bottom).

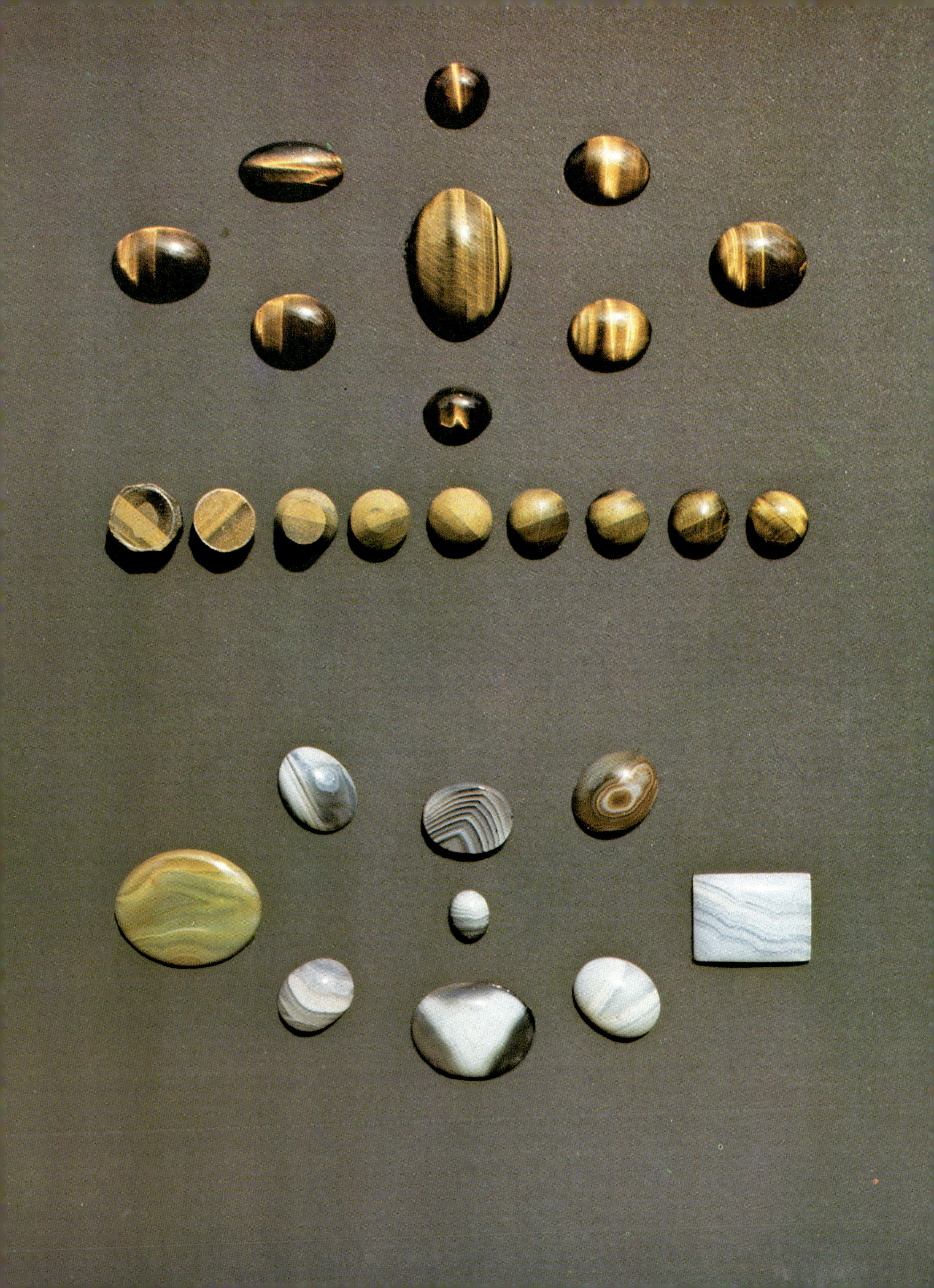

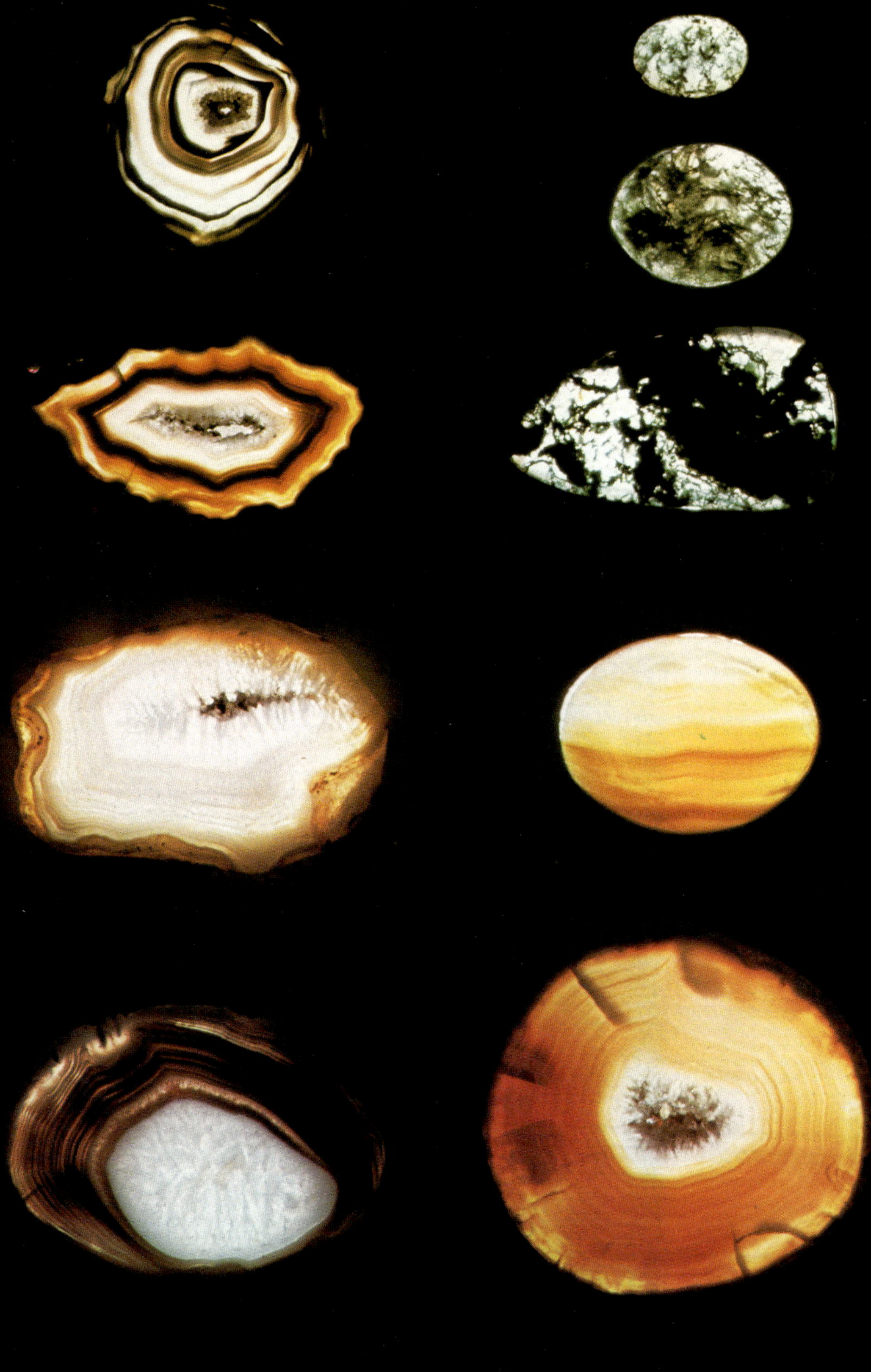

8. CUTTING A CABOCHON

It is generally recognised that any polished gemstone with a smooth, curved shape is said to be a cabochon. There are, however, several standard shapes of which ovals, circles, rectangles and pendants are the most popular. As well as the outline shape the cross-section is also grouped to give high, medium and low domed cabochons, depending upon their degree of curvature. The type of cross-section used depends a great deal on the character of the stone and on personal choice.

Selection of material

Careful selection of material for cabochons can save many hours of work and avoid disappointment. Nothing is more frustrating than to have a gem ruined in its later stages when careful examination of the slice would have revealed the flaw, although sometimes, when dealing with opaque rough, this kind of disappointment cannot be avoided as internal flaws cannot be seen. In general it is better to purchase rock that is sold specifically for cabochon work as opposed to tumbling.

Providing a saw is available, one large piece of rock when slabbed is likely to give more flawless areas than a selection of small ones, but it must be remembered that buying rock is

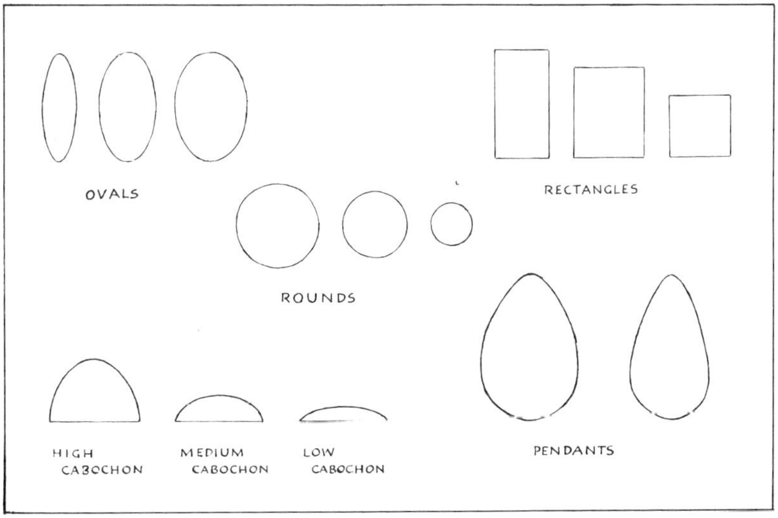

Fig 14 Selection of cabochon outlines and cross-sections.

Opposite: Mexican coconut.

always a gamble. Some which look promising from the outside, yield very little material that is worth working on, and others are the exact reverse; one of the most exciting things about lapidary work is cutting into the unknown, realising that no one else has seen what is about to be revealed.

Probably the best material for the beginner is one of the banded agates, preferably Botswana or Mexican, as these have a fairly high proportion of attractive banding. Agates are hard enough—about 7 on Moh's scale—not to work too rapidly, for while softer material is easy to work, it grinds so quickly it is very often difficult to control the shape.

Good rough must be solid, free from cracks and holes, and be uniform in texture: look closely, too, at the surface for signs of the rough being broken with a hammer, as it often has many small cracks beneath the points of contact. One quite useful test to see if the rock will take a high polish is to wet the surface and see how quickly the moisture soaks in, porous material, which is less likely to polish well, soaking up the moisture in a few seconds. This method can also be used for checking uniformity of surface to see if moisture soaks in more quickly in some places.

Sawing

The first cabochon attempted should not be so big that it takes a long time to finish, or too small so that it is difficult to hold. Elongated shapes should also be avoided, as these will present one or two problems for the beginner. A reasonable size to start with is a $\frac{3}{4}$in by $\frac{5}{8}$in oval, for which a slab about $\frac{1}{4}$in thick is suitable for a medium domed cabochon. The thickness of the

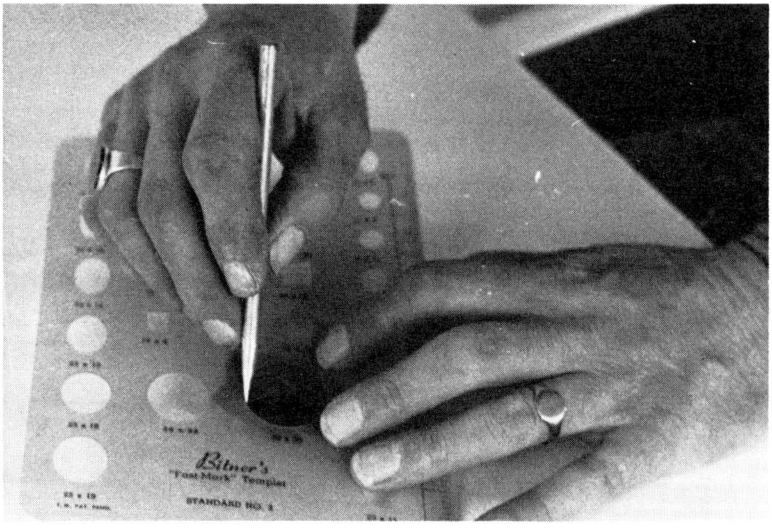

Plate 41 Use of marking template.

slices cut will vary from roughly $\frac{3}{16}$in to $\frac{3}{8}$in, depending on the size and dome on the finished cabochon. When cutting up a piece of rock, slices of different thickness should be prepared to cover all possibilities.

Once the slab has been cut wash it well with warm soapy water to remove all traces of oil. Break off with a pair of pliers any projections left from the saw, to enable the marking template to lie flat on the stone.

Marking out

Templates are used to mark the required shapes. These are flat sheets of clear plastic with calibrated and shaped holes cut in them. If the jewellery mount for the stone is to be made by hand, draughtsmen's templates can be used as the mount is made to fit the stone, but if it is intended to set the stone in a commercial mount, a metric stone template must be used.

Examine the slice very carefully for flaws and mark each one as it is found; if the stone is transparent or translucent hold it up to the light to see the flaws more easily. Lay the template on the stone and move the selected shape over the surface until the best pattern is found, and as the shape is to be marked on what will be the bottom of the cabochon, the other side must also be checked for pattern. The marking is done with an aluminium or bronze rod sharpened to a point; lead pencil is of little use because it will wash off easily and is not hard enough to give a thin line. Make sure the marker point fits right into the corner of the template, by leaning the rod at an angle as shown in figure 15 and Plate 41.

The aluminium or bronze pencils are not hard enough to scratch the stone, instead, a layer of metal is deposited, and since this can still be rubbed off, it must be protected with a coat of clear nail varnish.

If one side of a slice is uneven, or if the sample is very small and is difficult to hold steady for marking, it can be embedded in a piece of plasticine.

Trim sawing

When the varnish is dry the shape is roughly cut out with the trim saw. The table of the saw must be clear of any tiny chips of stone, thus allowing the slice to lie flat, since any wobble which is set up can damage the blade. Saw away as much of the waste as possible, but do not cut too close to the line. Remember to

Fig 15 Point must fit right into corner of template.

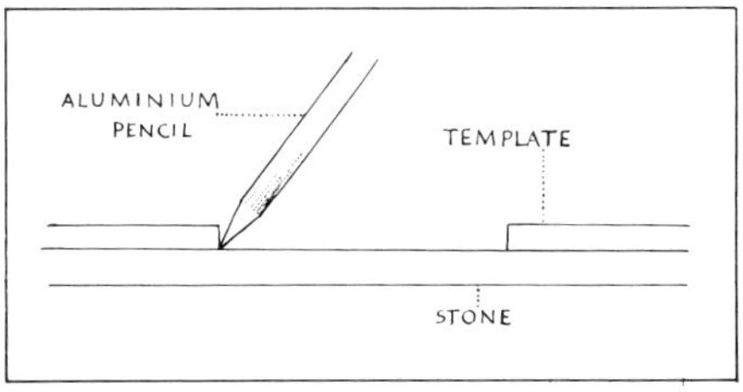

Fig 16 Trim sawn blank.

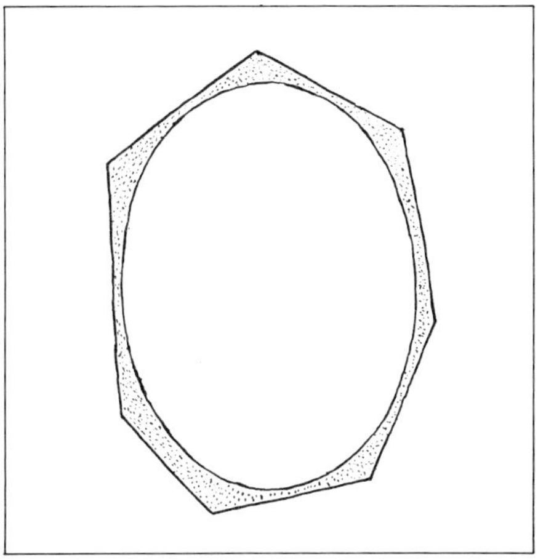

start all saw cuts at right angles to a side to form a notch, and then slowly turn the rock until it is lined up: the spray of oil being thrown off the blade gives a good indication of the position of the cut. It may even assist the beginner to draw a series of straight lines on the blank where the cuts are to be made.

Grinding the outline

Having washed the oil from the stone, it is now ready for grinding. Remember the sequence for grinding: switch the machine on; apply the water; grind; remove sponge or turn off water supply; leave wheel running to throw off water; switch off.

Hold the stone firmly, with the thumbs on top and the fingers underneath, resting the sides of the hands or the wrists on the trough for extra support. The marked side of the blank should be uppermost so that the line can be seen and any chipping that may occur will be on the eventual top of the stone—these indentations will be ground away when the top is being shaped. Move the stone gently forwards until it is just touching the wheel, and apply gentle pressure to start grinding.

The stone must be turned so that the ground edge follows the curved line, and one way of achieving this is to move one hand forward and the other backwards, allowing each end of the stone to pivot between the thumbs and fingers: then alternate the hand motion.

Try to avoid using the centre of the wheel face at this stage otherwise a hollow will form, and do not grind right to the line, leaving a band about $\frac{1}{32}$in wide around the oval.

Fig 17 Blank ground nearly to the line.

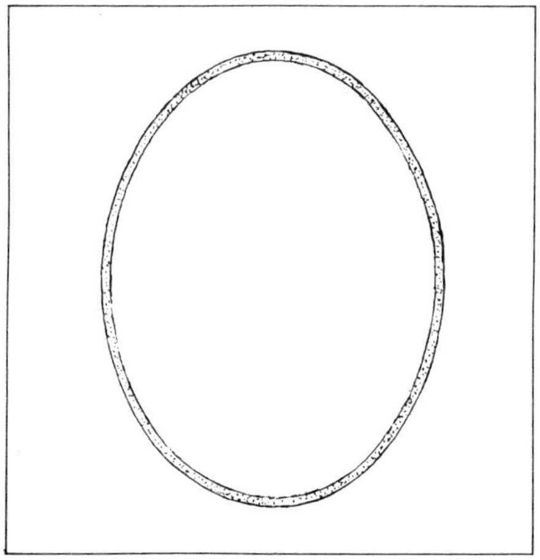

There are several reasons for leaving this band: no matter how accurate the marking, it has been done inside a template and is bound to be slightly undersize; later work on the stone is going to reduce the size slightly; and it is fairly easy to make a finished stone smaller but impossible to increase it.

Aim to grind the sides of the blank so that they are at right angles to the bottom of the stone: this means holding the blank so that the point of contact with the wheel is level with the centre of the shaft.

When this stage is finished use the side of the wheel to grind a very tiny bevel on the bottom of the blank, no more than $\frac{1}{16}$in across, to prevent the corner from chipping and also to assist if the stone is to be set into a bezel setting—a very tiny ridge of solder is often left in the corner of a bezel and the small bevel prevents the stone sitting on this.

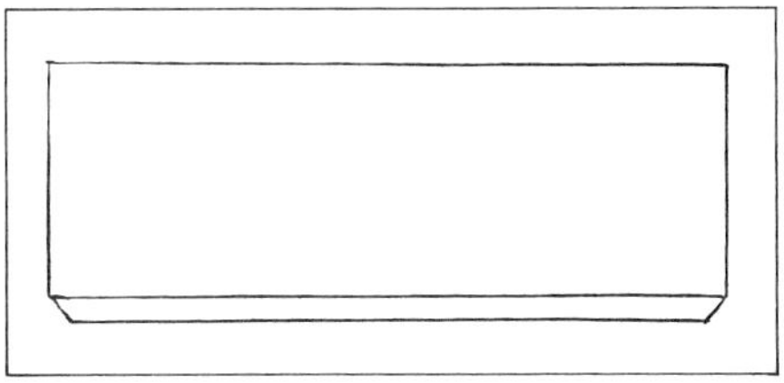

Fig 18 Small bevel ground around bottom edge.

To make for easier handling, the stone is now fastened onto a stick.

The dop stick

The object has this peculiar name, since the process of fastening the stone to the stick is known as dopping. Dop sticks are usually made from hardwood dowelling rods, available from any good do-it-yourself store. The rods are cut to lengths of anything from 2 to 5in, with one end square, the length depending on personal choice, some people preferring the dop to be short enough to fit into the palm of the hand, while others like it longer: it is best to try out several lengths to find out which is best suited.

After a little experience, most lapidaries work simultaneously on a number of stones, taking them together through each stage, for which a good selection of dop sticks is needed, ranging from ⅛ to ¾in diameter—in fact, ten to twelve of each size is not an unreasonable number.

Dop sticks are not exclusively made of wood, however, since large nails and bolts have been used successfully, but if one is going for metal dops, aluminium is probably the best as it does not rust. Metal dop sticks have the advantage of not absorbing water as do wooden ones, which can then expand and crack the dopping wax.

This wax is coated on the squared end of the stick to hold the cabochon in place. Most lapidary suppliers sell dopping wax and unless a great deal is needed it is hardly worthwhile making it up, but for those who wish to manufacture, the main ingredient is sealing wax, which is unfortunately far too brittle to use on its own. There are several other ingredients that can be added but the following routine and recipe has worked very successfully for many years.

Break up the sticks of sealing wax, place them in a tin and add five to ten per cent by weight of beeswax. Heat this mixture gently until melted, and stir until the two are thoroughly mixed; the heat may have to be increased slightly for this to take place.

Fig 19 Wax run down stick to form platform.

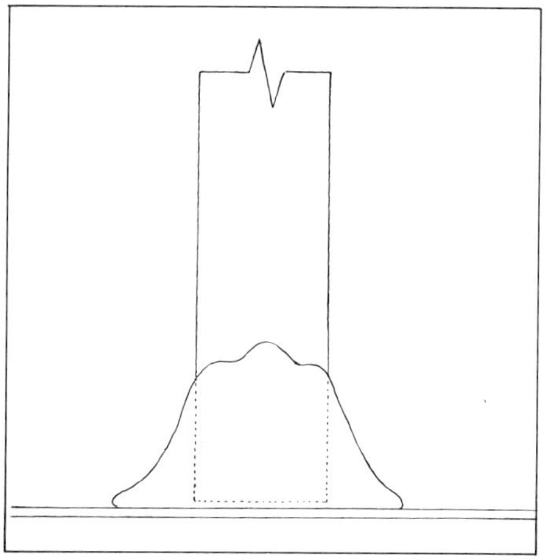

Fig 20 Tin can with side cut out.

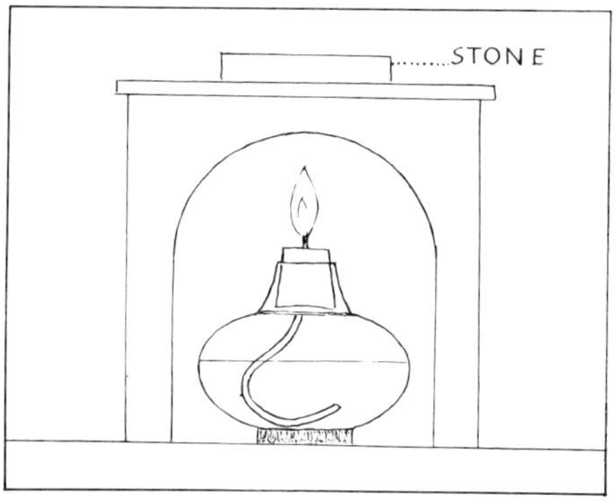

Opposite: Plate 42 Gemtek Dinky Dopper.

Remove from the heat and starting with the thinner sticks dip the end about half an inch into the liquid, stir once to pick up wax, lift out and stand the dop stick, wax down, on a smooth surface such as a sheet of glass, formica, or smooth metal. The wax will tend to run down the stick and spread out on the surface to form a platform.

Allow about 10 minutes for the wax to solidify, then tap the top of the stick sideways. If the amount of beeswax is correct the dop will break away fairly cleanly leaving a corner on the plate. If too much beeswax has been added the wax will bend and refuse to come away, while, if too little, the dop will not have stuck to the plate at all. The remedy is to re-heat the mixture, add more beeswax or sealing wax depending on the symptoms, and begin again. The larger dop sticks may require two applications to pick up sufficient wax.

Dopping

Having chosen a dop stick that is slightly smaller than the stone, thus allowing room for the wax, the stone itself must be heated slowly over a low flame: the secret of adhesion lies in putting a hot stone onto cold wax, not the other way about.

Plate 42 shows a commercial dopper, but as can be seen in figure 20 a tin box with the side cut out, or even a tin plate propped up on two bricks, will do just as well, with the heat coming from a candle, spirit lamp or jewellers torch.

Since the dop stick is to be fastened to the bottom of the stone the blank is placed onto the hot plate with the marked side uppermost. One flake of shellac, as used in making French polish, laid on the stone will not only indicate when it is hot enough but will help to give a stronger bond.

As soon as the flake begins to melt remove the source of heat— do not leave it until the flake has completely melted otherwise the stone will be too hot. Roll the waxed end of the dopstick in the flame to soften the wax, then press it firmly and vertically onto the centre of the stone, getting stick and stone in contact since too much wax between them will weaken the bond.

Check that the dopstick is centrally mounted and upright and that the wax has flowed slightly to cover the bottom of the specimen—occasionally this does not happen and the wax must then be moulded to shape with a wetted finger. Never attempt this with a dry finger as hot wax can remove the skin. There is no need to hurry when dopping as the stone retains its heat for many minutes.

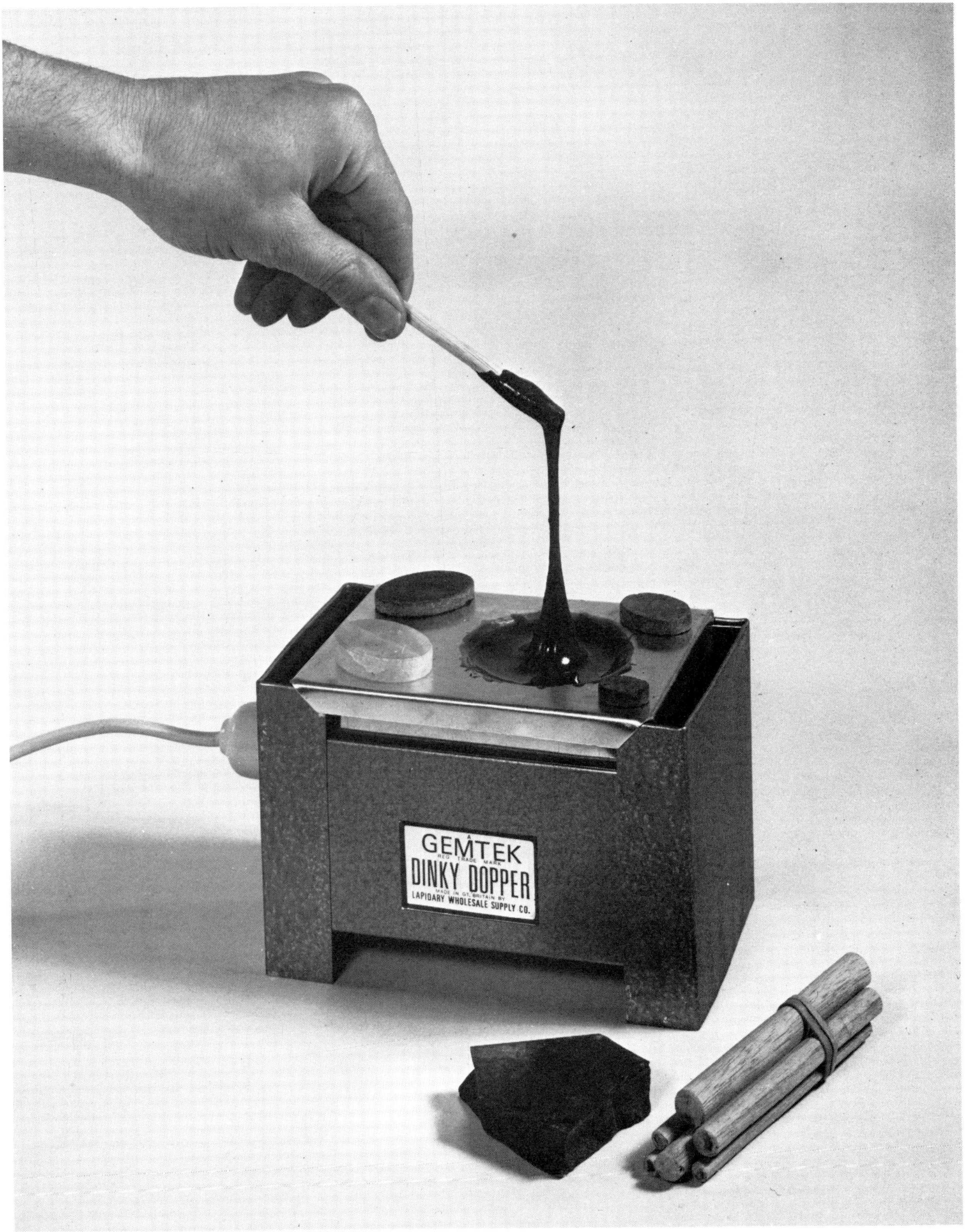
GEMTEK
REG. TRADE MARK
DINKY DOPPER
MADE IN GT. BRITAIN BY
LAPIDARY WHOLESALE SUPPLY CO.

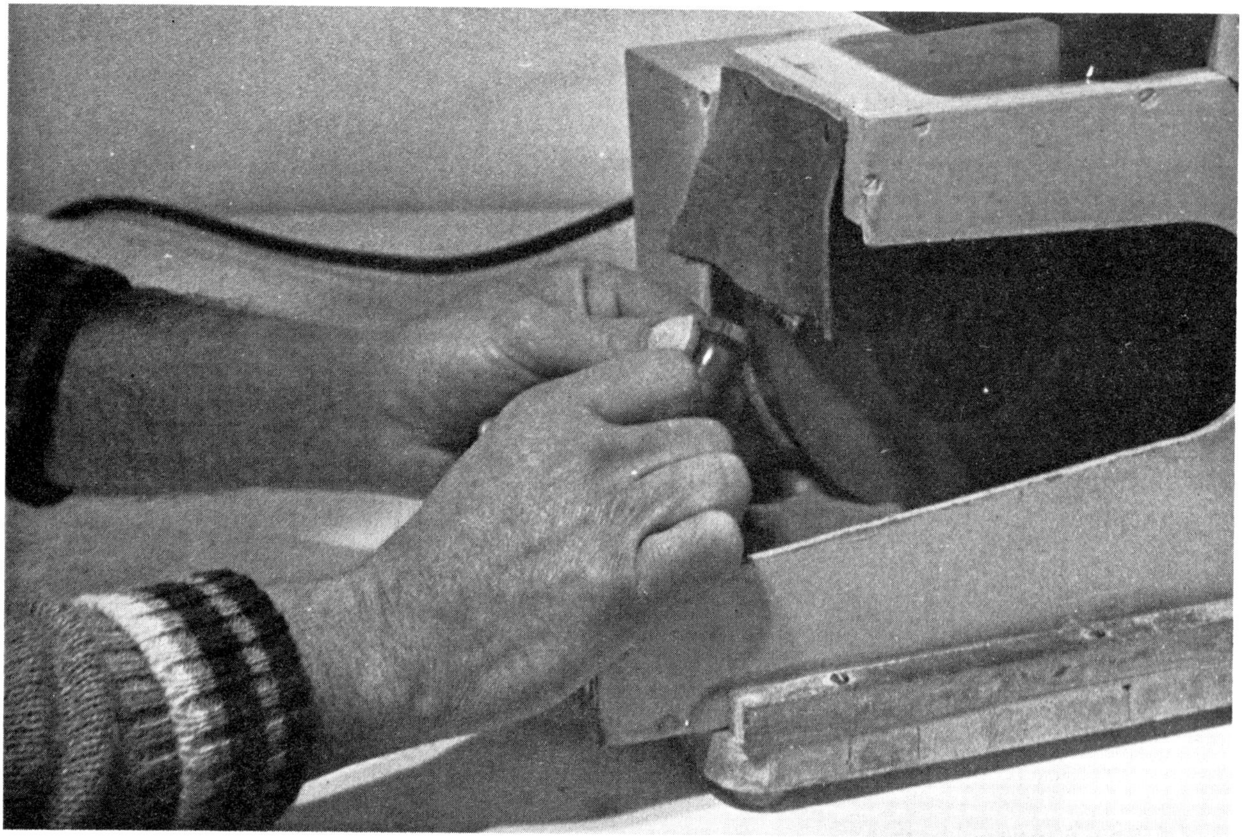

Plate 43 Holding dopped stone to grinding wheel. Note position of thumb and fingers of the left hand.

Fig 21 Stone properly mounted on the dopstick.

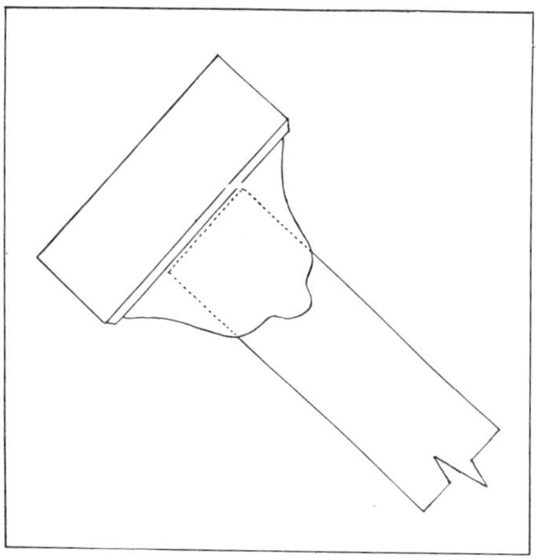

Grinding the curve

When the stone has properly cooled—don't try to speed this up by immersing in water as the stone will come off—wax that has run down the edges must be scraped away with a penknife: it is important that the bottom corner of the stone is visible at all times.

Hold the stone and dop stick as shown in Plate 43, remembering that the stick is only an aid; if it is held in both hands and pressure applied to the stone, it will come off. The left hand, supporting the stone, applies the pressure and the right hand holding the dop stick imparts a twisting action. The stone is gently and slowly swept diagonally across the face of the grinding wheel. The aim now is to grind a broad bevel sloping in from bottom to top at an angle of 10 to 15 degrees, an angle which is fairly critical for a bezel setting because the metal is pressed onto this slope to hold the stone in place. If it is too steep the stone will not be held firmly; if too shallow, the metal will wrinkle when worked down. Starting work at the top corner of the stone, gradually work the bevel down to within 1/16in of the bottom.

The bevel must never touch the bottom corner of the stone as this would alter the shape of the outline.

The next step is to grind a second bevel at 45 degrees, this one being taken roughly half way down the first. The flatter and more accurate these bevels are ground the easier it is to obtain a symmetrical curve. Large, low-domed cabochons will need subsequent bevels at lower angles.

The final stage of grinding the top is to turn the series of bevels into a continuous curve. Hold the dop stick between the fingers and thumbs of both hands, rotate it rapidly, and allow the stone to gently 'tick' against the grinding wheel. Start with the dop stick at right angles to the face of the wheel, then gradually lower the angle until it is about 10 degrees to the face. Do not take the angle lower than this, or the bottom corner will be ground.

Return slowly to the original position and repeat the operation until a perfect curve is formed. This curve will grow fairly quickly and a continuous check must be made on it, looking at the side and end so that the shape of the dome can be seen. The two main errors the beginner is likely to make are in a slightly lop-sided curve, or a flat top, as shown in figure 24.

The remedy for the first defect, quite obviously, is to grind more from the high side of the curve, and for the second, to grind a bevel around the top corner. It is essential not to have even a small flat on the top of the dome as it will be impossible to remove it in later stages.

Coarse sanding

Dry the stone thoroughly and examine the surface, which should be covered with coarse scratches from the grinding wheel, every one of which must now be removed on the 220 grit sander, one scratch missed ruining the final polished surface. A new 220 sanding disc will cut very rapidly, so until it is broken in, only light pressure will be required; as the operator becomes more proficient greater pressure can be used to speed up the sanding, but one must always remember that the greater the pressure, the quicker the stone will heat, therefore plenty of water should be used, and the stone kept moving continuously. A 220 grit is still coarse enough to remove a lot of stone if it is held in one position for as little as two seconds, resulting in a small flat.

The ideal procedure is to hold the dop stick in one hand as close to the stone as possible, rotate it backwards and forwards

Fig 22 Grinding the first bevel.

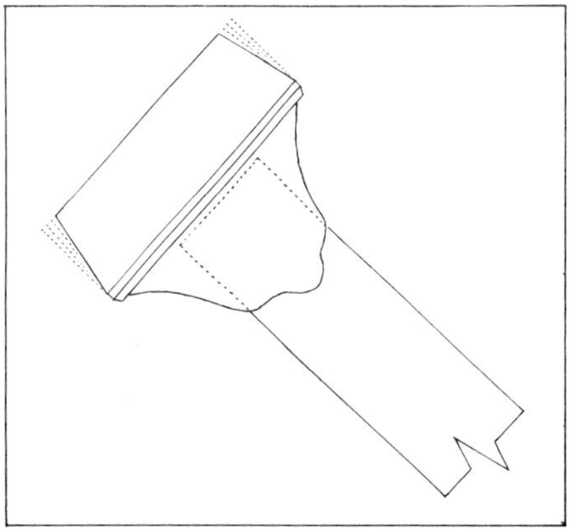

Fig 23 Second bevel ground halfway down the first.

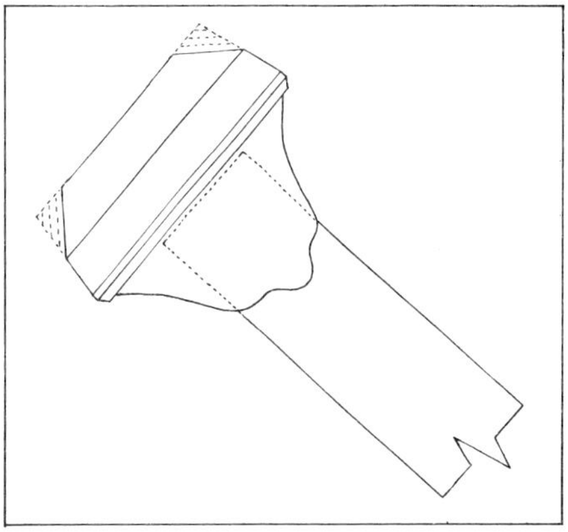

Fig 24 (a) Perfect curve (b) lop-sided curve (c) flat top.

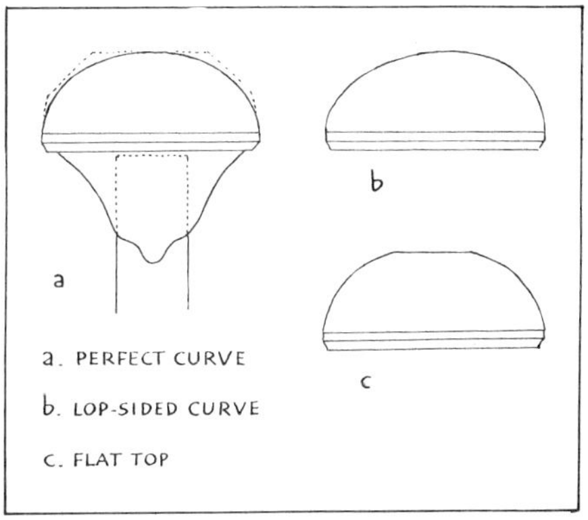

between the thumb and fingers and keep altering the angle of the stick to the face of the sander. This method is particularly useful for softer stones which sand rapidly, but harder rocks can be sanded with a slower, stroking action. Try to sand the edges of the stone first, gradually working in towards the centre. Since a disc sander moves quicker at the edges than at the centre, this can be used to regulate the speed of sanding, however, all stones that undercut should be sanded towards the edge of the disc using plenty of water.

Dry the stone again to examine the surface—this cannot be overemphasized as it is so important, even a very slightly damp surface being capable of hiding scratches.

Medium sanding
When perfectly satisfied that all the grinding marks have been removed, change to the 320 sanding disc. At this stage if there are one or two small flats on the surface, the 320 sander is the final chance of removing them. The method of sanding is exactly the same as before, but the checking may not be quite as easy: until the eye has become accustomed to picking out the difference between 220 and 320 scratches it is advisable to use an eye glass.

Fine sanding
The procedure is the same again, using 400 grit which is fine enough for most stones. The speed of cutting is so slow that much pressure can be used. When finished, the gem should show a glossy surface covered with very tiny scratches that are difficult to see, although as on some varieties of stone, 400 scratches tend to show up more, it is then advisable to use a 500 or 600 grit for a final sanding.

Polishing
Wash the hands and stone, paying careful attention to the wax behind the stone. Select the correct polish, mix a small quantity and apply it sparingly to the revolving buff, enough to keep the felt damp but not wet.

Polish the edges of the cabochon first, holding the dop stick in one hand with the forefinger on one edge to apply the pressure. Roll the stone until a small section is perfectly polished, turn it and overlap onto the next section, repeating until the whole edge is polished. Now raise the angle of the dop stick and continue polishing in concentric bands until the whole surface is done [Plate 44].

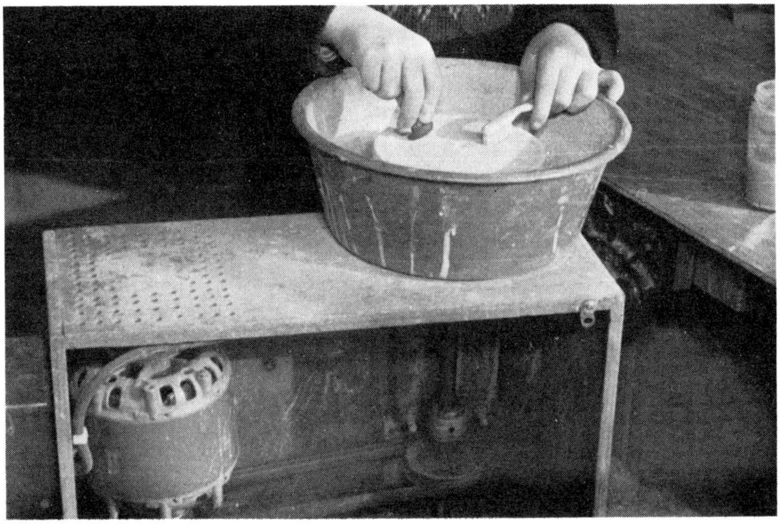

Plate 44 Holding dopped stone for polishing.

Rapid polishing needs firm pressure to build up the necessary friction, but frequently testing to prevent overheating. The gemstone should be held so that it is dragging on the buff to avoid the edges catching.

The surface should be wiped with a soft tissue throughout the operation to inspect the results, and the finished gemstone examined carefully as described in Chapter 5. Assuming the gem has been properly sanded the usual mistakes in polishing are the result of insufficient checking, resulting in areas that have been missed, not enough pressure being applied, or the buff being too wet or too dry. The remedies are obvious.

There are several ways of removing the stone from the dop stick: heat the wax and push the stone off with a matchstick; heat a thin knife blade and slide it between the wax and the stone; or place stone and stick in a freezer compartment or refrigerator for a few minutes and then separate them with the thumb.

Some larger stones can be pushed straight off with thumb pressure, but all these methods leave wax on the gem, which can be scraped off with a penknife or softened in alcohol and then wiped off.

The back of the stone needs to be flat for fitting into a bezel setting, and transparent and some translucent stones are better if the bottom also is polished, which can be done very quickly on a lapping machine or a sheet of glass. Finally if the stone is too big for the setting it can be made smaller by removing material from the bottom using either the side of the grinding wheel or the flat lap.

Doublets and triplets

As the name suggests, these are stones made up of two or three pieces. Some very attractive stones are very difficult or impossible to polish, while others, such as Opal, occur in very thin seams and cannot be used unless made into a doublet.

Basically there are two kinds of doublet—one, as used for Opal, where a piece of similar rock is cemented to the back for strength, and the other where a piece of clear Quartz is cemented onto the face. A triplet is a combination of both these—similar rock on the back and a Quartz lens, as it is sometimes called, on the face.

Precious Opal is found in thin seams, sandwiched between a colourless Opal called potch. The potch is ground away to reveal the colour, the surface of which is then lapped flat using 500 grit on a sheet of glass. Dark potch or black Obsidian to be used for the background is also lapped flat, and the two surfaces are cemented together. A Quarts lens can be cemented onto other rocks in a similar way, but being harder it will have to be flattened using coarser grit and ending on the 500.

Clear epoxy resin is ideal for cementing the surfaces together. Clean the surfaces first with acetone, warm the two pieces of rock, smear both with resin to which the catalyst has been added, and bring them together using firm pressure and marry them with a sideways, sliding movement to exclude all air and excess glue. A spring clothes peg can be used to keep the two together until set, when the stone is ground and polished in the usual way.

A sobering thought to finish on is that with reasonable care, the polish on the gemstone will last for many thousands of years.

9. TUMBLING

Tumbling is the easiest, and initially the cheapest, method of obtaining an abundance of polished gemstones. Machinery can be quite inexpensive and is so simple that a homemade machine can be produced quite easily. Basically, tumbling consists of putting rough pieces of stone into a barrel with abrasives and water, and turning it until the stones are ground perfectly smooth. The unusual, and very often attractive, shapes obtained by this method, plus the fact that very little attention is required, make an excellent introduction to lapidary work. The shapes produced create a challenge to find a suitable method of setting, and have produced many varied results, ranging from the use of simple epoxy resin to more complex wires, claws and collets.

The main principle of tumbling is to rotate the barrel at a speed where the stones are carried up one side, turn over at the top, and then slide to the bottom. This continual sliding gradually wears away both the stone that is sliding and the others it is sliding over.

Barrels

A shallow, large diameter barrel will grind stones quicker than a deeper one with a smaller diameter, because more stones will press on those underneath and increase the abrasive action. The size of the barrel chosen will depend upon the size and number of stones to be polished; if only a small quantity is needed a 6in barrel should be large enough, however, a school or club tumbler will require a larger barrel of about 12in. Practically any container can be used, as long as it is watertight; one where the top can be removed easily and resealed is better for de-gassing. It is advisable to open the barrel after the first three or four hours of tumbling, and then every two days, to allow any gases formed to escape: if this is not done they could build up in sufficient quantity to explode the barrel. A simple barrel to make is shown in figure 26.

The advantage of this arrangement is that by increasing the length of the bolts, two barrels can be used with the addition of one disc. See figure 27.

Fig 25 Principle of tumble polishing.

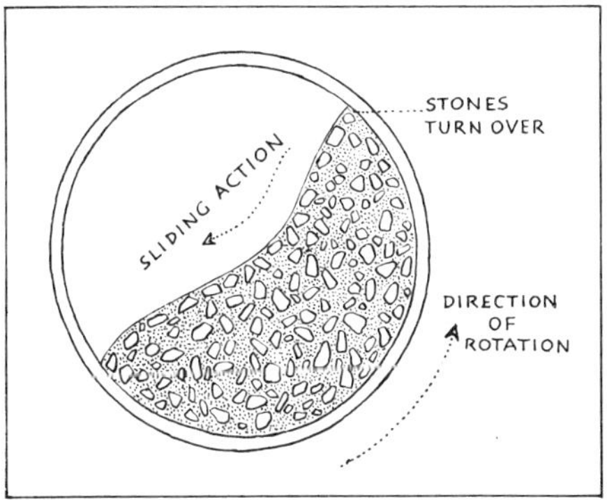

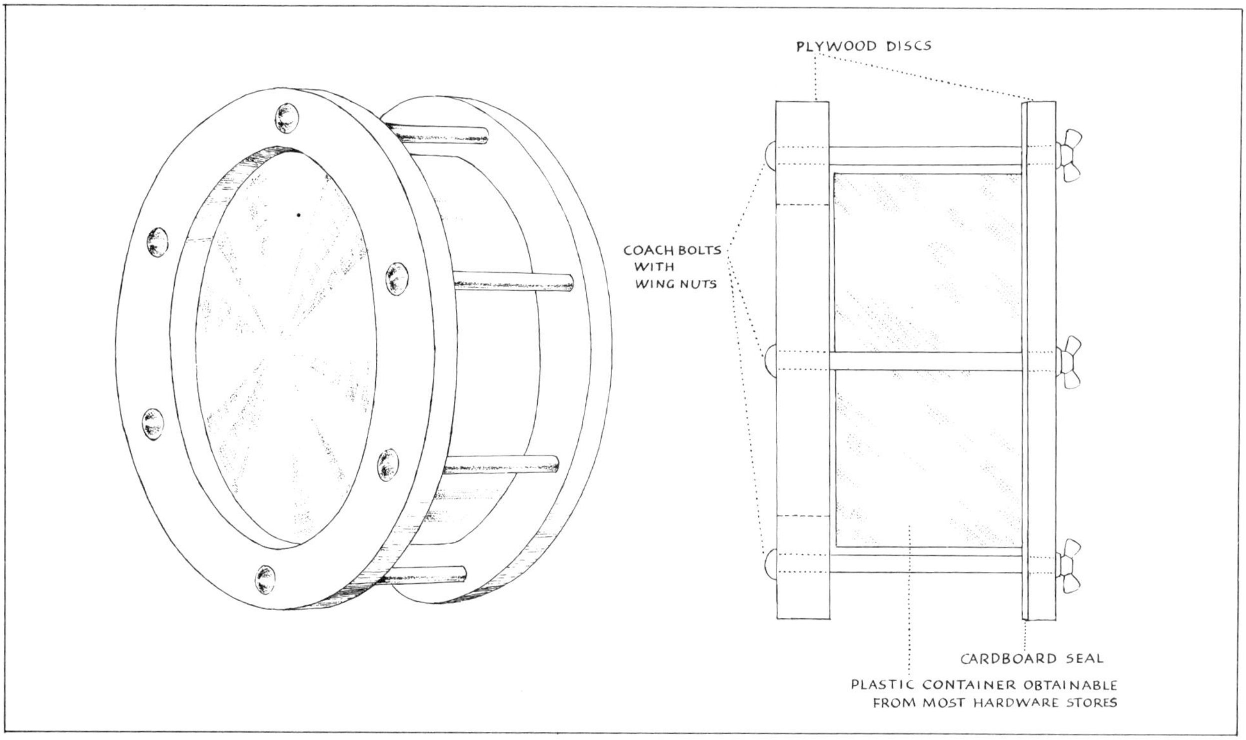

Fig 26 Home-made tumbler barrel.

A large hole can be cut in the bottom disc to act as a window; although this is not essential, it is fascinating to actually see the tumbling action, and it provides a useful check to see if the speed is correct.

Tumbling machines

The basic design for a tumbling machine is shown in figure 28. The rollers should be made of steel covered with a rubber sleeve to provide friction; rollers from an old clothes wringer are excellent if a fairly large machine is envisaged. Bearings can be simple brass sleeves, or ball races, inserted into wooden blocks, or more sophisticated plummer blocks can be purchased. The easier the rollers turn the less load on the motor and the cheaper it will be to run. At one end of the driving roller a large pulley is fitted and connected to the motor by a vee belt. A secondary drive from the opposite end of the driving roller to the idling roller can be used, but is not essential. All pulleys can be stepped to provide different speeds for different barrel sizes, but provision would have to be made for adjustment of the distance between the rollers. A selection of commercial tumbling machines is shown in Plates 45-48.

Tumbling speeds

To obtain the best results, the speed at which the barrel turns should be fairly accurately determined: a tumbler that is rotating a little too fast will take the stones too far up the side, and instead of turning over and sliding down, they will fall quite heavily upon one another. This is likely to cause cracking and chipping, and should be avoided. A still greater speed will result in centrifugal force plastering the stones onto the tumbler wall with little or no grinding taking place. On the other hand, speeds that are too slow will result in the contents being taken only a little way up the side and the whole load sliding back again in one mass. One advantage of the plastic barrel already described is that the action can be observed and the speed altered to obtain the maximum abrasion.

When the load cannot be seen, it is possible by listening carefully to hear if the speed is correct. If it is too fast there may either be no noise at all because centrifugal force is preventing any movement, or it may be very noisy where stones are falling on one another. Too slow a speed will cause an intermittent swishing sound as the whole load slips backwards. The correct speed should cause a continuous swishing, murmuring sound as the stones are taken up, fall over and slide down. The following table is a guide for barrel speeds.

Diameter of barrel	r.p.m.
6in	35-55
10in	25-40
12in	15-25

Fig 27 A twinning arrangement.

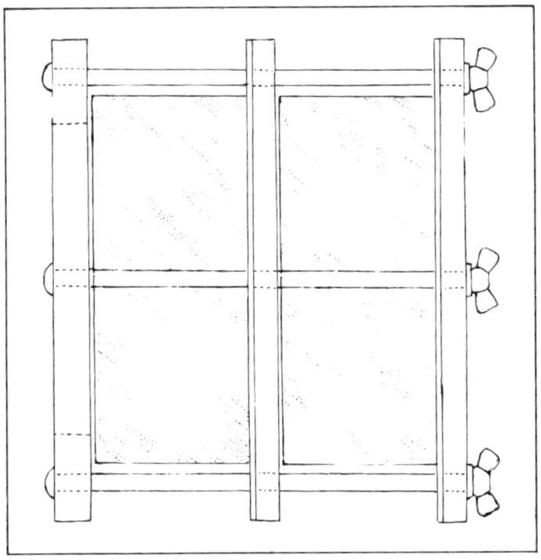

Fig 28 Tumbler: basic design.

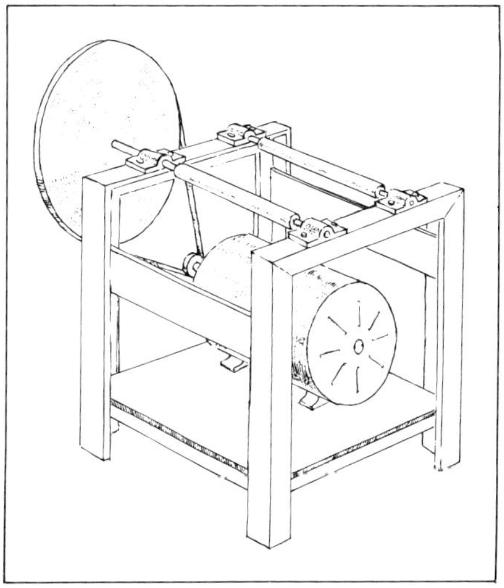

Selection of material

Ideally, material of the same size and hardness should be placed in the barrel. If soft material is mixed with hard it will be ground away very rapidly, even to the point of vanishing completely. Brittle stones mixed with tough will shatter easily and large mixed with small will grind at different speeds.

Stones with deep cracks or holes should be discarded or broken into smaller pieces as there is a chance of grit being lodged in them and contaminating finer grinding. Above all, remember that tumbling will not turn into something of great beauty a stone that is not good enough for a cabochon.

Preparation of material

The easiest way to break stone is to use two cold chisels. Fix one upside down in the vice, hold the stone in position with the second chisel on top and hit it with a hammer. In most cases the stone will split in the correct place, if the two chisels are lined up. Another method is to cut the rock into thick slabs with a

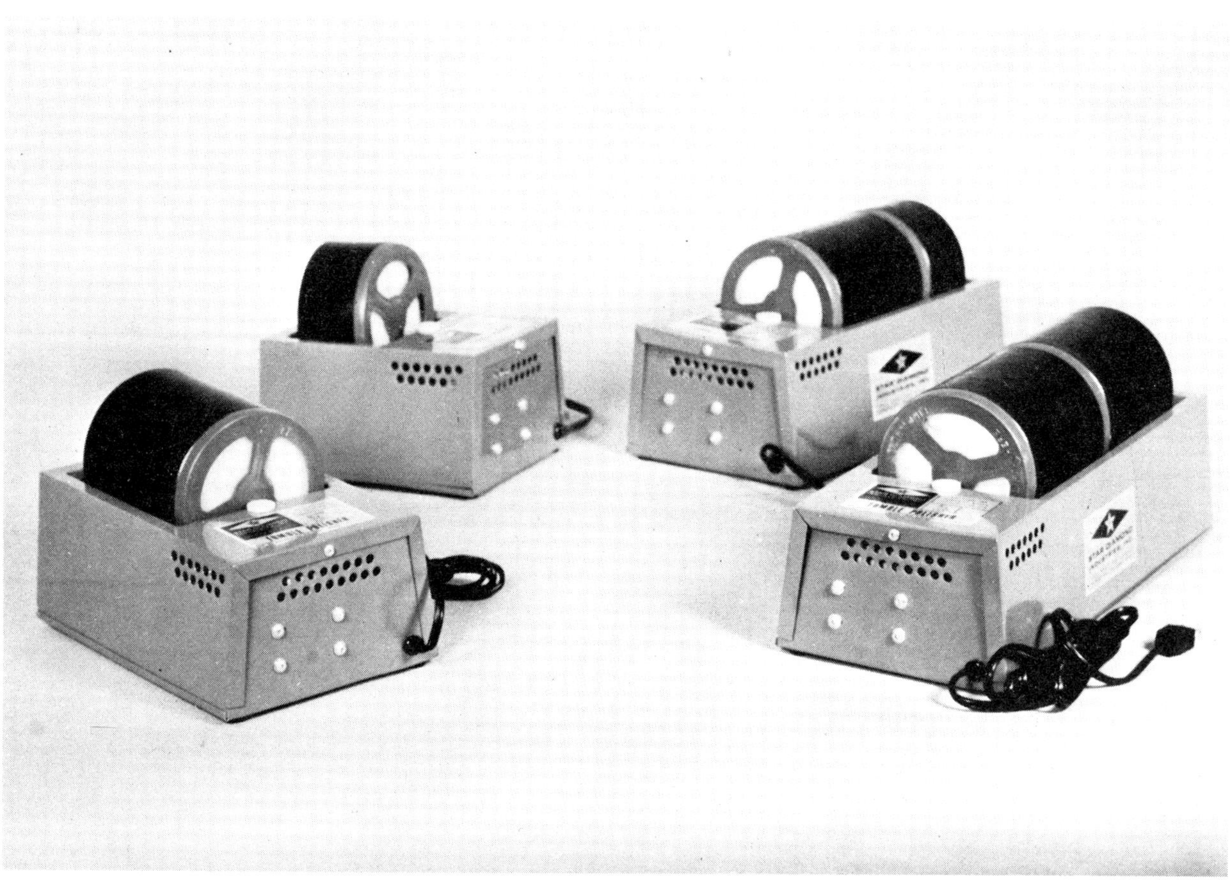

Plate 45 Selection of Star Diamond tumblers.

slabbing saw and then break them with a hammer. Many dealers also sell selected tumbling rock which has usually been crushed to a uniform size. Small pieces of waste from sawing can also be kept until sufficient is available to make up a charge for tumbling.

It is possible to grind away unwanted protrusions, holes, and cracks on a wheel before tumbling, to cut down on the polishing time; this is such a laborious process that it is always advisable to think well ahead. A final tip to avoid last-minute changes of mind: whenever a rough piece of rock is selected for tumbling, grind it at once. Do not leave it until there is sufficient material to fill the barrel or the job may never be done.

Charge size and abrasive

The barrel should be charged to between half and threequarters of its volume with stones and abrasives, with enough water added to just cover the charge. The amount of stone is fairly

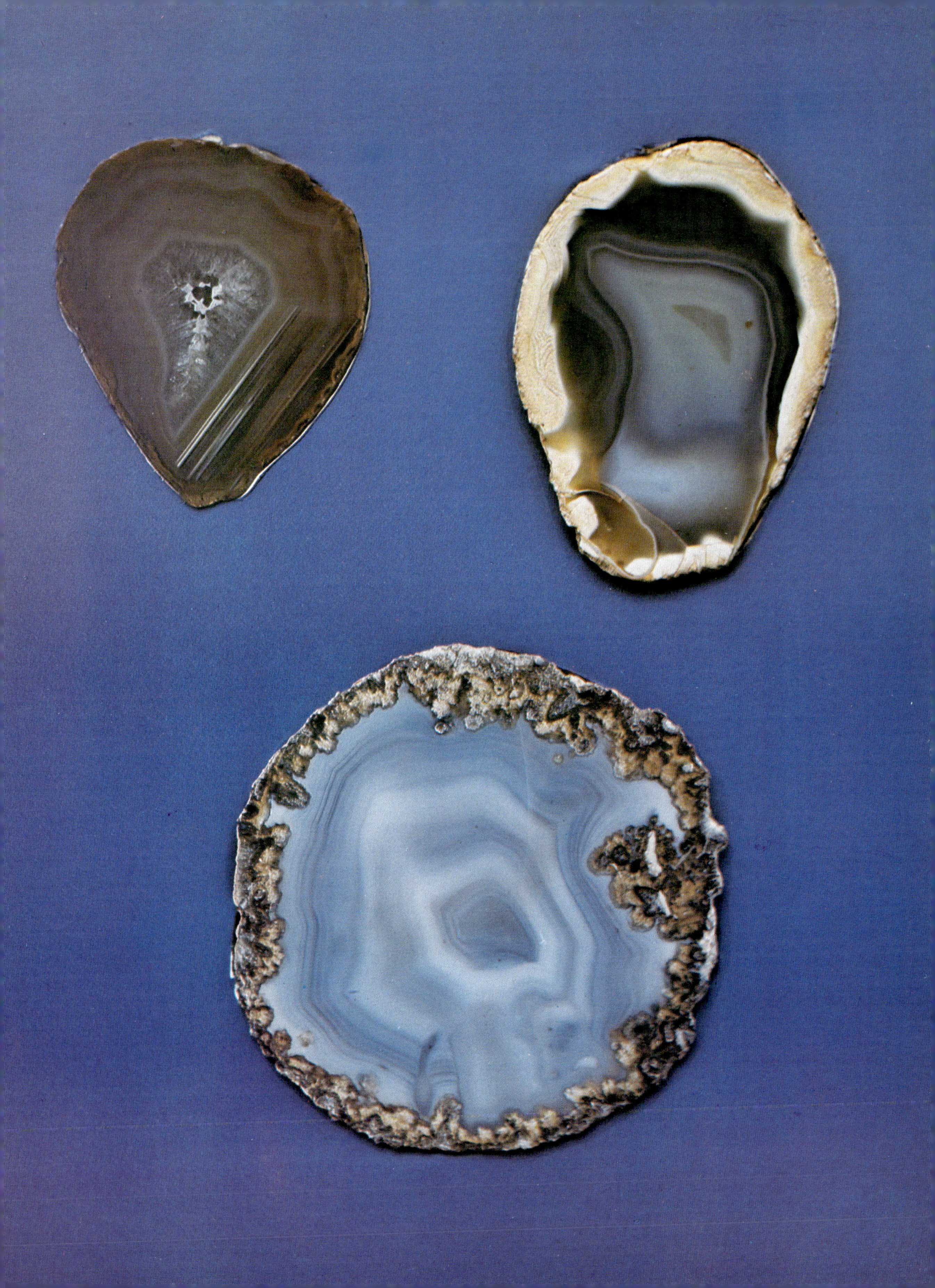

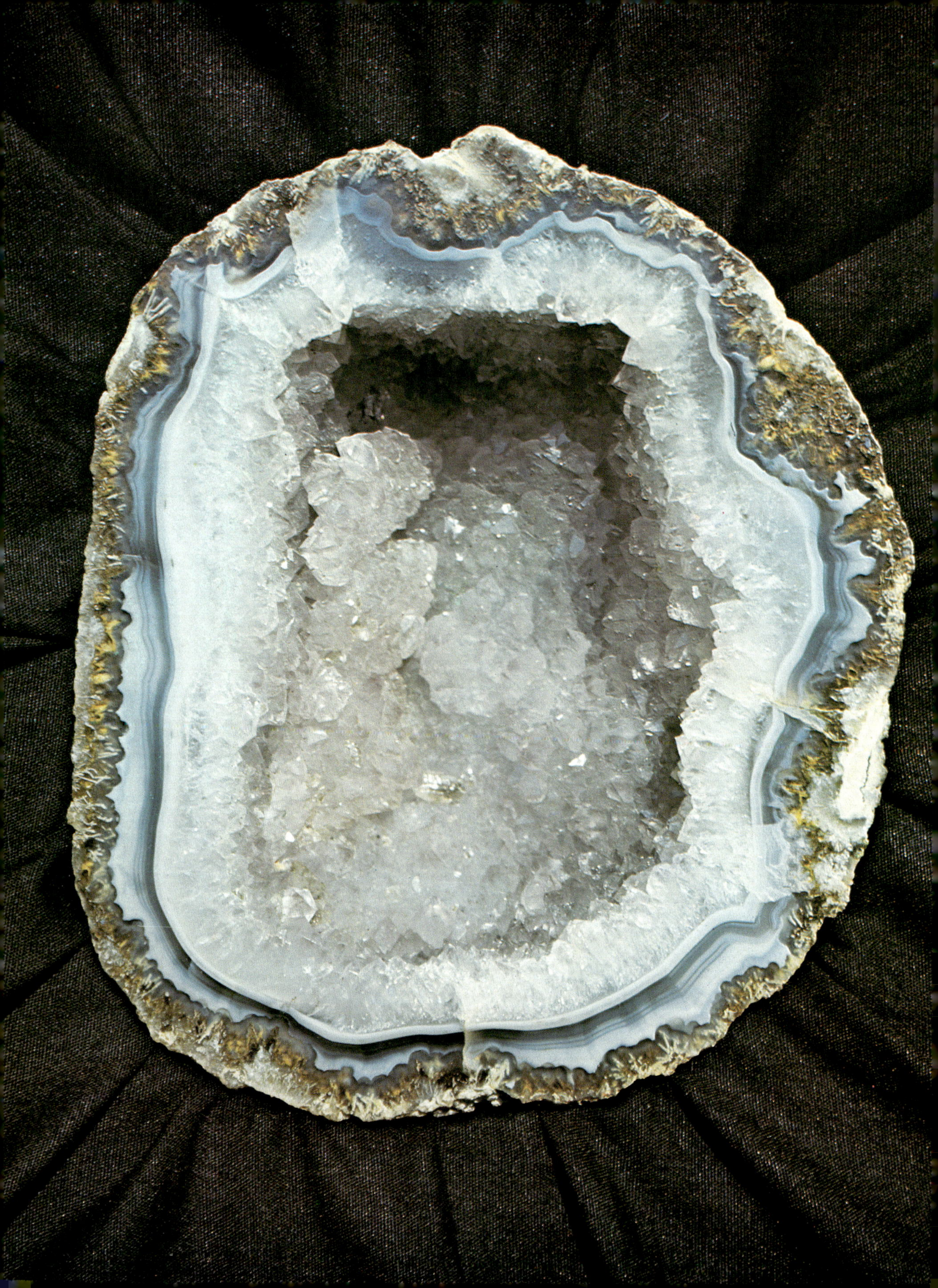

critical, too large a load not giving a steep enough slope for the sliding action to take place, and too light a load causing the whole charge to remain practically stationary with very little grinding happening, except to the wall of the barrel which will wear rapidly.

The abrasive used for grinding is silicon carbide. A coarse grit, 60 to 80 mesh, is used for the first grind, and 500 mesh for the second. Intermediate sizes of grit can be used, but if the first grind is carried out properly they are not necessary. Old silicon carbide grinding wheels can also be used in the first grind; broken into one inch pieces they will assist with the grinding, as they erode, further particles are added to the charge.

The ratio of grit to stone for the first grind by weight is about one to three parts of abrasive to ten parts of stone, the larger amount used for harder and tougher stones, the smaller for softer ones. Faster grinding is obtained if the charge is washed every two or three days and the grit renewed. This will be very costly but the job can be done satisfactorily using only one or two changes of grit.

Tumbling times

The first grind usually takes from one to four weeks of continuous grinding 24 hours a day. This time obviously varies according to the size, shape and hardness of the stone, and the size and speed of the barrel, and there is no hard and fast rule

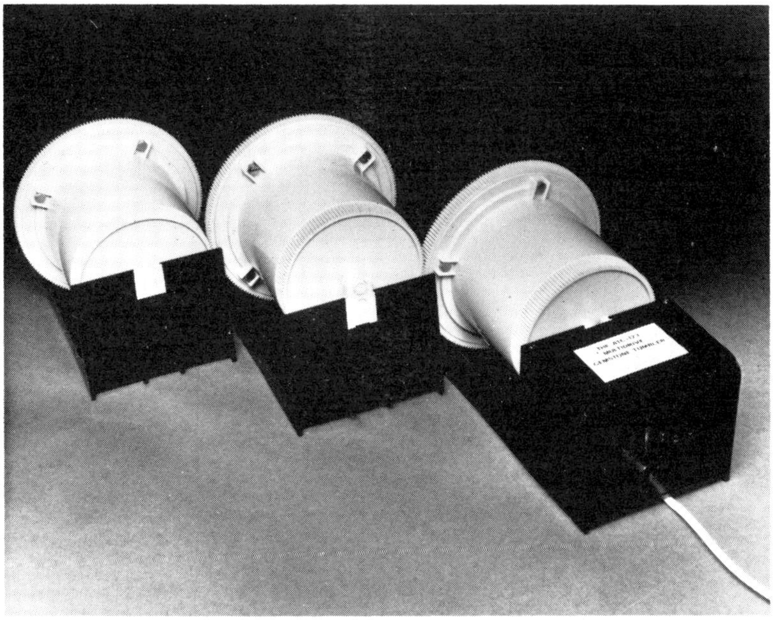

Plate 46 The Wessex ATC-123 tumble polisher. A multi-speed tumbler using one driving unit and others mesh into it.

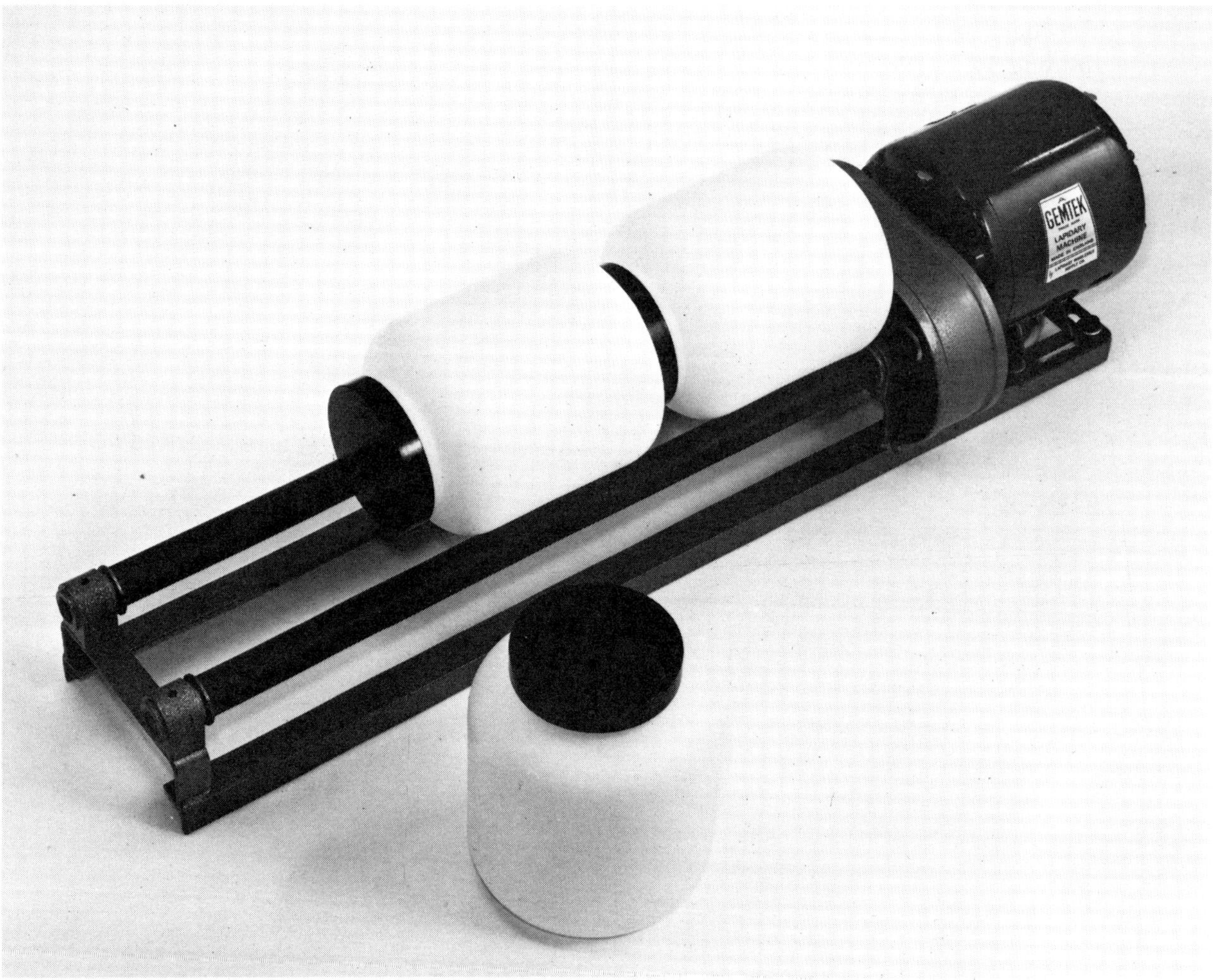

Plate 47 The Gemtek three-barrel tumbler.

that can be laid down. Examination of the charge every two or three days is the best way of checking the time needed, and stones that are smooth and have no pitting can be removed to avoid overgrinding, although the weight of stone lost in this manner must be made up to keep the grinding action correct.

Material to make up the loss can be obtained in several ways. Smooth and uninteresting pebbles can be collected especially for this purpose, remembering to keep size and hardness about the same. With the final stage of polishing completed ruthless sorting out is in any case essential to maintain a high standard, and the rejects can then be used as makeweights. Other stones which have internal holes and flaws that are not visible until the surface has been ground away, should also be removed at the end of the first grind and kept for makeweights. When inspecting the charge always take a fairly large sample, wash and dry it thoroughly, as the stones look better when wet. Inspection is also important because prolonged grinding will tend to produce flattish stones.

The stage will eventually be reached—on the first attempt this will seem like a lifetime—when all the stones have been satisfactorily ground. The barrel and the stones must then be thoroughly washed to ensure that no particles of grit are carried forward to the fine grind. It is very important to remember that at no time should grit or rock dust be washed down the drain as it will very quickly settle and clog the waste pipes.

The barrel is re-charged with the stone and 500 grit, plus sufficient smooth material to make up the amount lost in grinding the first stage, which can be as much as twenty per cent. One way of allowing for the loss of weight is to use two barrels for the first tumble and select enough stones from both for the fine grind.

Plate 48 TP2 3lb British tumbler.

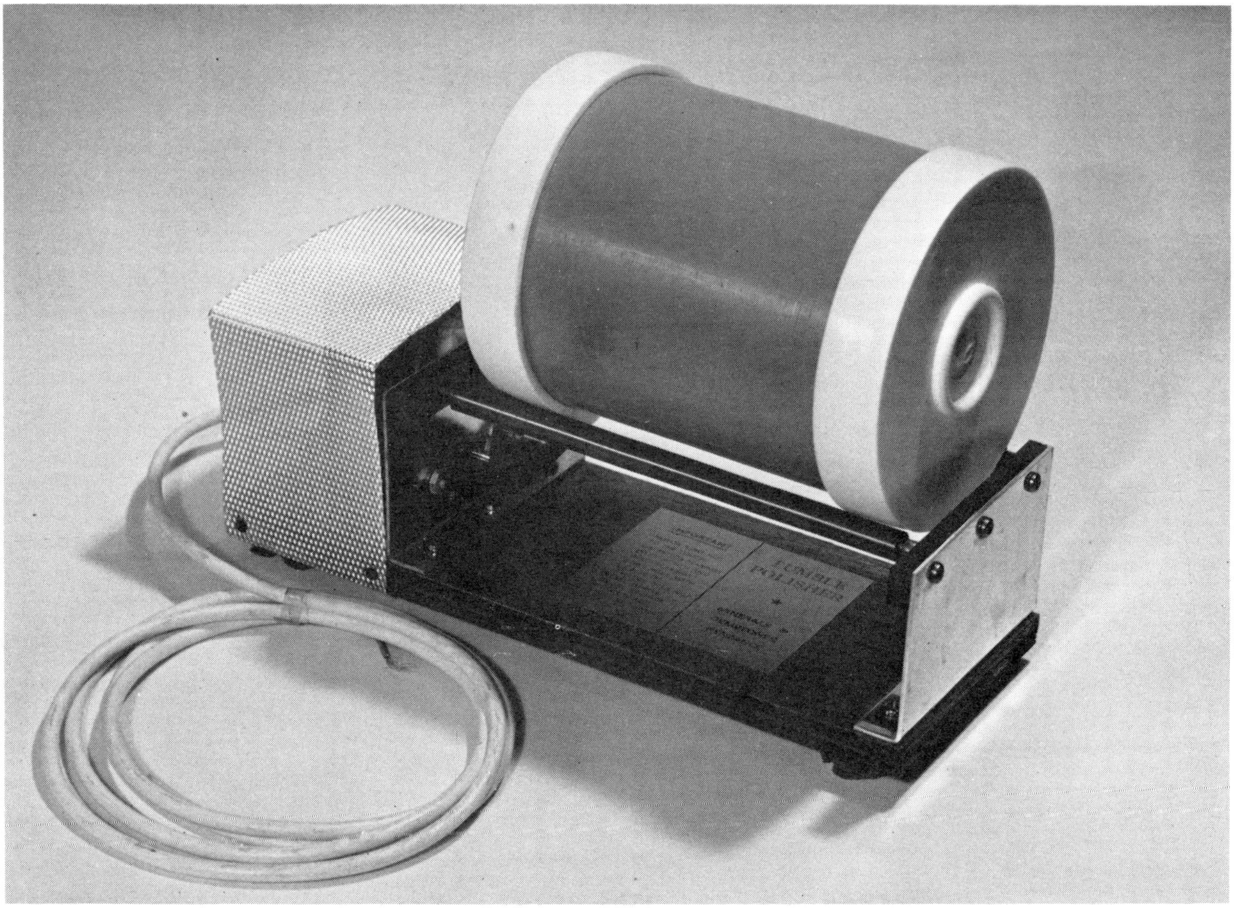

This stage takes about one week, checking frequently to see if the surface has been worn fine enough; a stone selected at random will come up very quickly on a polisher if the coarser grinding marks have all been eliminated. If a polisher is not available, the stones will have to be examined with the aid of a magnifying glass. Any scratches still left from the 80 grit will be easy to distinguish from those from the finer 500 grit. One coarser mark means going back to tumbling with 500 grit.

Polishing

When the stones have been thoroughly washed replace them in the barrel with either tin or cerium oxide and water. Of these two, tin oxide seems to give the better results for tumbled stones. Additives either of cubes of hardwood, pieces of felt, or leather should be added to the charge to give a cushioning effect whilst tumbling. These will help prevent chipping of sharper edges and points and also act as a polisher when rubbing against the stones. If leather is used, thick pieces are better than thin, as the latter tend to cling to the barrel and not mix with the stones. The ratio of the mixture is about ½lb of tin or cerium oxide and 2lb of additives to 10lb of stone. Polishing will take four to five days, or even up to a week. Inspection should still be carried out regularly, since if any sign of frostiness is present no amount of polishing will remove it. Frostiness is a sign that insufficient time has been spent on the fine grind, and this should be done again.

Tin and cerium oxide are both expensive materials and should be reclaimed for future use by washing the stones so that all the water runs into a large clean container. Allow the mixture to stand for a week or two, when all the fine powder will have settled. Syphon off the water from the top, collect the residue and store it in a dustproof container.

A final burnish may be imparted to the stones by tumbling for two or three hours in a very thick mixture of detergent water and sawdust, which will also clean the stones thoroughly.

10. THE MORE COMMON GEMSTONES AND THEIR TREATMENT

Some of the materials dealt with in this chapter are not gemstones in the strict sense of the word, as they are not durable enough to be used for jewellery. But they are capable of being polished.

The hardness given is the standard Moh's hardness as given in most textbooks.

Agates Hardness 6.5-7 Specific Gravity 2.65
Agates, a member of the Quartz family, are formed in ancient lavas in almond-shaped cavities created by the expansion of gases in the molten rock. When the rock was subsequently decomposed by circulating water, the minerals present were broken down and the solutions formed deposited their charge in the cavities. The Agate so created, may have inclusions which give a spotted or patchy appearance, or sometimes look like ferns or trees. If the cavity is only just lined, other mineral solutions may percolate through and form subsequent layers, giving rise to a banded Agate.

No two Agates have been found alike; each is unique in shape, pattern and colour and because of this are probably among the most exciting of stones to cut. They range in size from pieces weighing a few grams to huge boulders of several hundredweight.

Agates are usually named after their place of origin—Brazilian, Australian, Scottish, Botswana—and American Agates after the state or district, hence Montana, Wyoming, Death Valley, etc. There are many varieties and names used but the main types are:

Banded Agate. Fine concentric bands of varying colours. The more vivid contrasts, found in some polished stones, are usually a result of artificial colouring. A form of banded Agate where the bands make very angular turns and look like the plan of an old fortress, is termed 'fortification Agate'.

Agates with inclusions. These can be transparent, translucent or opaque with inclusions forming in different ways. The Agate is named after the appearance of the inclusion, hence:

Moss	clear Agate with moss or fern-like inclusions.
Dendritic	tree-like inclusions.
Plume	billowing feather-like inclusions.
Flower	like clusters of flowers.

Most varieties of Agate are very tough and not sensitive to heat, although care has to be taken when grinding to avoid corners chipping. The lapidary should always examine the slice very carefully for flaws and break the rock along them before marking out, as the cracks do tend to creep when the specimen is heated.

Agates respond very well to polishing with cerium oxide on felt, but some, such as moss, turritella, and blue-lace, sometimes have tiny holes that fill up with polish which is difficult to remove. An examination of the surface before marking out may avoid this; or the holes may be filled with epoxy resin before the final sanding.

Alabaster Hardness 2 Specific Gravity 2.3
A compact form of gypsum which is very soft and can be cut very easily with a hacksaw. Use either a fine grinding wheel or a 220 sanding disc for shaping, but even a fine disc will remove material rapidly. Is best polished by hand using a damp piece of leather with tin oxide or silver polish.

Amazonite Hardness 6 Specific Gravity 2.56
One of the feldspars and rarely found in crystals, it is mostly massive, and a fine green to bluish-green, sometimes with white flecks. It has pronounced cleavage planes and low-domed cabochons should not be attempted as they will easily break. The rock is not heat sensitive and can be polished well with cerium oxide and felt.

Amber Hardness 2.5 to 3 Specific Gravity 1.05 to 1.10
Amber is not a stone but is of organic origin, being the fossilized resin from coniferous trees growing in Lower Tertiary times, and occasionally small insects are found entombed in it. If rubbed on a piece of wool it becomes electrified and will pick up tiny pieces of paper. The colour ranges from pale cream through to reddish-brown and is usually transparent to

translucent. Very sensitive to heat, Amber will soften at 160°C and melt above 250°C. It is also soft enough to cut and shape with hand saws and files and polishes well on very damp leather with cerium oxide. Cabochons are best shaped on hard-backed sanding discs using plenty of water.

Amethyst Hardness 7 Specific Gravity 2.65
Amethyst is a clear, coloured, quartz, varying from pale violet to deep purple, even within one small piece, and the deeper the colour the more expensive the specimen becomes. Needing careful examination as flaws are difficult to see, it is not sensitive to ordinary dopping temperatures but can lose its colour if subjected to slow strong heat; moderately heated it will turn yellow. Cut and polish as for Agate.

Apatite Hardness 5 Specific Gravity 3.2
Transparent to translucent yellowish green, this is an attractive stone but is brittle, weak and contains many flaws. Much care is needed when dopping as it is extremely sensitive to heat—use shellac instead of wax for dopping. Sawing, grinding and sanding must be done carefully finishing with a worn 500 grit disc. Polish with tin oxide on leather.

Aragonite Hardness 4 Specific Gravity 1.6
White to grey, sometimes banded; brittle and heat sensitive, Aragonite can be dopped in the normal way providing it is heated gently. Sand on worn discs and polish with tin oxide on soft leather.

Aventurine Hardness 7 Specific Gravity 2.65
A member of the quartz family containing many small flat plates of mica which give a gold-spangled effect, it is usually green or blue and works fairly easily, although some undercut may occur when sanded too slowly. Polish with cerium oxide on felt. Aventurine glass is an artificial stone made from ready fusible glass containing flakes of copper and is sold as 'Goldstone'.

Barite Hardness 3 Specific Gravity 4.5
A massive, rather soft material, it ranges in colour from nearly white to dark brown. Some interesting banded varieties are available resembling wood grain. It is very sensitive to heat but can be dopped with care, but low domed cabochons are not recommended as the stone is very brittle. The dark brown banded variety polishes well on felt with cerium oxide.

Beryl Hardness 7½ to 8 Specific Gravity 2.68 to 2.90
The gem varieties of Beryl are: Emerald, characterised by its beautiful green colour; Aquamarine, in which the tint varies from pale-blue to greenish-blue; Yellow Golden Beryl, and pink Morganite. Ordinary Beryl is an opaque blue-grey, blue, yellow or white. All varieties are tough, very heat resistant and polish well on hard felt with cerium oxide.

Bloodstone Hardness 6½ Specific Gravity 2.6
A crypto-crystalline form of quartz, the dark green colour is due to inclusions of green earth. This stone is also known as Heliotrope. Look for pieces with clear red spots and avoid those with lighter green patches as they are usually soft and do not polish well. Polish as for Agate.

Calcite Hardness 3 Specific Gravity 2.71
Calcite is more often used in its impure form of crystalline limestone with other minerals, when it is called Marble, but there is a transparent variety known as Iceland Spar, which gives double refraction, and an opaque, white to yellow-brown variation. All may be treated as for Alabaster.

Carnelian Hardness 6½ Specific Gravity 2.6
A translucent crypto crystalline quartz varying in colour from pale flesh to deep wine, it produces beautiful cabochons which need to be sanded on 600 grit. Polish as for Agate.

Chalcedony Hardness 6½ Specific Gravity 2.6
This occurs as botryoidal (having a surface like a bunch of grapes) and stalactitic translucent masses and is usually greyish or bluish. Same treatment as for Agate.

Chrysoprase Hardness 6½ Specific Gravity 2.6
Chrysoprase is Chalcedony stained green with a hydrated compound of nickel, and needs gentle heat when dopping otherwise it may lose its colour. Always use new discs for sanding to avoid undercutting; polish on leather with tin oxide.

Citrine Hardness 7 Specific Gravity 2.65
A member of the quartz family varying in colour from pale to deep orange-yellow, it provides excellent material for cabochons, tumbling and faceting, but the deeper coloured material is best for cabochons as the lighter rock will appear colourless. Polish as for Agate.

Garnet Hardness 6½ to 7½ Specific Gravity 3.6 to 4.2
Garnet, the name commonly given to a family of minerals, is usually associated with the colour red, but can be green, yellow, crimson, brown, white, orange or colourless. Most gem Garnet is transparent except Grossularite, which is translucent. Fairly heat sensitive, but able to withstand normal dopping temperatures, most Garnets are fairly brittle and care must be taken to avoid chipping the edges. The final sanding should be on a worn 500 disc; polish on leather with chrome oxide.
Main gem types are: —

Almandine	deep red, sometimes with tinges of purple.
Andradite	deep green to yellowish green.
Grossularite	yellowish-red to honey-yellow; green massive material from South Africa is known as 'Transvaal Jade'.
Pyrope	fine blood-red. The South African variety is falsely called 'Cape Ruby'.
Spessartite	usually red, stones with a good colour are rare.

Granite
A coarse textured igneous rock containing visible Quartz, Feldspar and coloured minerals, usually mica. The coarse texture makes it very liable to 'pitting' unless great care is taken when sawing and grinding, but very attractive large cabochons can be made and are best polished on hard leather or wood, with cerium oxide.

Hematite Hardness 6 Specific Gravity 4.9 to 5.2
A red oxide of iron that is very messy to work with, though it presents no problems in sawing and grinding. Sand with a worn-out fine disc and polish with cerium oxide on leather or wood.

Jasper Hardness 7 Specific Gravity 2.65
A massive, compact quartz impregnated with much impurity, usually clay and iron oxide, Jasper is opaque and its normal colours are red, green, yellow and brown. More troublesome to work than Agate, due to its soft and porous patches, rough stone should always be tested by wetting and any pieces with high water absorption discarded. Polish with cerium oxide on felt; if this fails use Linde A with leather.

Jet Hardness 3 to 4 Specific Gravity 1.3
Greatly worked in the last century for 'mourning' jewellery, Jet has very similar properties to Amber and can be worked in the same way. Polish by hand with cerium oxide on soft leather.

Labradorite Hardness 6 Specific Gravity 2.7
Probably the most attractive of the feldspars when properly cut, when first viewed it appears as a dirty grey, slightly greasy rock. If correctly orientated it shows flashes of brilliant peacock blue, green, yellow, red and orange, but orientation is difficult and is best done by wetting the rock, holding it directly under a light, and turning it until the 'labradorescence' shows: the stone is then cut parallel to the colour. If the slice has to be tilted to obtain the play of colour another cut will have to be made adjusting the angle of the cut. Slices need to be thicker than normal as it cleaves easily, and flatter domed cabochons will show the colour better. Polish on hard felt with cerium oxide.

Lapis Lazuli Hardness 5½ Specific Gravity 2.7 to 2.9
Best quality material is of a deep, intense blue and comes from Afghanistan. Poorer qualities have white or grey patches. Iron pyrites are very often present and careful sanding is needed to prevent these protruding from the finished surface. Polish with chrome oxide or Linde A on soft leather.

Laurvikite Hardness 6 Specific Gravity 2.7
A medium textured igneous rock mainly of feldspar, when polished it shows a pale blue flash. Found mainly as an ornamental stone and for shop fronts, it is also useful material for the beginner as many offcuts can be obtained from stone masons. Fairly strong and heat resistant, it polishes well on felt with cerium oxide.

Malachite Hardness 3½ to 4 Specific Gravity 3.9
A very attractive, brilliant green stone with banding of dark and light greens sometimes showing interesting circular patterns. Good rough comes from Zaire and is relatively expensive. It is fairly heat sensitive but careful dopping can avoid fracturing; great care needed when grinding to obtain a symmetrical curve as it is so soft, and thin slices should be avoided as it is rather brittle. Best sanded with worn discs and plenty of water. Polishes well on felt with cerium oxide providing it does not get too hot.

Marble Hardness 3
True Marble is metamorphosed limestone and can be treated the same as Alabaster. Many attractive, so-called Marbles contain fossils and are really very compact limestone and are worked in the same way.

Moonstone Hardness 6 Specific Gravity 2.57
Good quality, transparent material showing a blue flash comes

from Sri Lanka and is difficult to buy in the rough. This again is a feldspar, and the greyish, opaque material is uninteresting to look at until correctly orientated. Working procedure is the same as for Labradorite.

Obsidian Hardness 5 Specific Gravity 2.4
A volcanic glass formed when lava is chilled quickly. Usually black, it can be red or brown; black material with white patches is known as Snowflake Obsidian. Care is needed when grinding to avoid chipping, and final sanding should be on a worn 600 disc. Polish on felt with cerium oxide.

Opal Hardness 5 Specific Gravity 1.9 to 2.2
Opal is a very widespread, common rock; unfortunately it is only the gem variety that is worth cutting, and this accounts for a very tiny percentage of the Opal available. Precious Opal owes its great beauty to the fantastic play of colour shown when light falls on the surface of the stone, blues, greens, reds and oranges being the predominant colours.
The main gem varieties are:

Black Opal	almost opaque with a deep blue to almost black background showing a range of brilliant colours.
White Opal	white background with play of colour, with blue and green the main colours.
Fire Opal	transparent to translucent variety, reddish-brown to orange. Usually faceted as play of colour is not always present.
Jelly Opal	transparent opal, almost colourless showing play of colour.

Some Opal show colour only after being immersed in water, and this temporary effect vanishes when the stone is dried for a few days. Heat is probably the greatest enemy of Opal since it destroys the play of colour by the expulsion of water contained in the rock. The temperature must be raised very slowly when dopping, using shellac, or if really careful ordinary dopping wax. Provided precautions are taken to avoid overheating there are no problems in working Opal, and it polishes well on felt with cerium oxide. Water should be used for sawing instead of oil, which can stain the stone.

Quartz Hardness 7 Specific Gravity 2.65
There is an abundance of ordinary milky Quartz found as white pebbles on many beaches. It polishes well but is uninteresting unless other minerals are present, such as the attractive cabochons which can be made from milky Quartz having bands

of smoky Quartz, Amethyst or Citrine running through it. This needs to be cut parallel to the band so that the crystal shapes are outlined on the surface of the cabochon. Treat as for Agate.

Rhodochrosite Hardness 3½ to 4½ Specific Gravity 3.5
An opaque material banded in deep and pale pink, it is difficult to control the shape when grinding and sanding due to the varying hardness in the bands. Sharp discs are needed for sanding to prevent undercutting; polish on soft leather with tin oxide.

Rhodonite Hardness 7 Specific Gravity 3.4 to 3.68
The fine grained massive form is tough and cuts fairly well, and is not heat sensitive. The rose-pink colour is attractive and the deeper coloured material takes a better polish. Use new, sharp discs for sanding to avoid undercutting, and polish with tin oxide on leather.

Rock Crystal Hardness 7 Specific Gravity 2.65
Rock Crystal is a clear, colourless Quartz, the most common of the crystalline varieties. Crystals vary in size from pinhead to those measuring a yard or more in length. Originally used for carving small ornaments before glass was produced, its main use today for the lapidary is the lens for doublets. Grind and polish as for Agate.

Rose Quartz Hardness 7 Specific Gravity 2.65
Rose Quartz is a delicate pink and always appears slightly milky; there is a tendency to lose its colour on exposure to heat or strong light. It is very difficult to obtain flawless pieces. Cabochons need to be reasonably high domed to retain depth of colour. The same treatment as for Agate but with careful dopping as too much heat can mean loss of colour.

Rutilated Quartz Hardness 7 Specific Gravity 2.65
A clear Quartz containing sparkling needles of rutile, and sometimes called 'Venus hair stone'. Best cut, if possible, with the needles parallel to the surface as tiny holes can appear when the ends of the needles penetrate the surface. Treatment as for Agate.

Serpentine Hardness 2½ to 4 Specific Gravity 2.5 to 2.65
Found in many parts of the world in a range of colours—reds, greens, and browns—often forming attractive patterns. It is easy to work, but plenty of water must be used for sanding, finishing on a worn 600 disc. Best polished by hand using crocus powder or compound on corduroy.

Smoky Quartz Hardness 7 Specific Gravity 2.65
A Rock Crystal coloured pale brown, almost to black, the very dark stone is called Morion, the reddish-brown stone found in Scotland is known as Cairngorm. Usually faceted, it can be cut into very nice cabochons. Treat as for Agate.

Sodalite Hardness 6 Specific Gravity 2.3
A massive, deep blue material streaked with white, it can be brittle, but is fairly easy to work and polishes on felt with cerium oxide.

Sunstone Hardness 6 Specific Gravity 2.65
A pinky-orange feldspar showing a golden flash when correctly orientated. Same treatment as for Labradorite.

Tiger Eye Hardness 7 Specific Gravity 2.65
Probably the most popular member of the Quartz family, it is a fibrous Quartz of a golden yellow-brown which gives a beautiful chatoyant effect—bands apparently moving across the stone when moved. Tiger Eye owes its origin to the infiltration by silica of Crocidolite, a blue fibrous asbestos. Oxidization of iron has given the brownish colour and when this has not taken place the stone is a greenish blue. Red Tiger Eye has been artificially coloured by heating and this is the reason why so much of this material is badly flawed. Most Tiger Eye cuts and polishes easily, though occasionally a piece will tend to undercut. This can be avoided by using new, sharp discs for sanding. Polishes very well on felt with cerium oxide.

Topaz Hardness 8 Specific Gravity 3.5 to 3.56
Transparent to translucent crystals, either colourless, pale blue, pale yellow or deep orange yellow—which is the colour usually associated with Topaz. Rose Topaz, which is pink, is formed by heat treating yellow stone. Often found as tough, heat resistant pebbles, Topaz is usually faceted, and will polish well on hard felt with cerium oxide.

Tourmaline Hardness 7 Specific Gravity 3.0—3.15
Usually found in long crystals with deep striations running along the sides, it comes in many colours including red, blue, green, brown and pink, and can be found with two or more colours in the one specimen. The commonest form is black, which is not used as a gemstone. Fairly heat sensitive and brittle, care must be taken when grinding to avoid chipping. Polish on leather with Linde A or chrome oxide.

APPENDICES

Appendix 1
Table showing shaft r.p.m. using various pulley combinations

Motor pulley at 1425 r.p.m.	Shaft pulley sizes 2in	2¼in	2½in	2¾in	3in	3½	4in	4½in	5in	6in	8in
2in	1425	1266	1140	1036	950	814	712	633	570	475	356
2¼in	1603	1425	1282	1129	1068	916	801	712	641	534	400
2½in	1781	1583	1425	1295	1187	1017	890	791	712	593	445
2¾in	1959	1741	1567	1425	1306	1119	979	870	783	653	489
3in	2137	1900	1710	1554	1425	1221	1068	950	855	712	534
3½in	2493	2210	1994	1813	1665	1425	1246	1108	997	831	623
4in	2850	2533	2280	2072	1900	1628	1425	1266	1140	950	712
4½in	3206	2849	2564	2331	2137	1832	1603	1425	1322	1068	801
5in	3562	3166	2850	2590	2375	2035	1781	1583	1425	1187	890

Shaft r.p.m.

Appendix 2
Table showing shaft r.p.m. needed

Diameter	Rim Speed 1,000	2,000	3,000	4,000	5,000	6,000	7,000
2in	1,910	3,820	5,730	7,640	9,550	11,460	13,340
4in	955	1,910	2,865	3,820	4,775	5,730	6,685
6in	635	1,275	1,910	2,550	3,185	3,820	4,455
8in	475	955	1,430	1,910	2,385	2,865	3,340
10in	380	765	1,145	1,530	1,910	2,290	2,675
12in	320	635	955	1,275	1,590	1,910	2,230
14in	275	545	820	1,090	1,365	1,635	1,910
20in	190	380	575	765	955	1,145	1,335

Shaft r.p.m.

Appendix 3
Metric Conversion Table

At the time of writing, imperial units are generally used in lapidary. For those who would prefer to work in metric units, however, the following equivalents are given:

¼ inch	6.35 mm	1 oz.	28.35 gm
½ inch	12.7 mm	1 lb.	0.45 Kg
1 inch	25.4 mm		
6 inches	152.4 mm		
1 foot	0.304 m		

LIST OF SUPPLIERS

The following is a list of firms who supply lapidary machines, materials and rough rock.

Ammonite Ltd., Llandow, Cowbridge, South Glamorgan.

Avon Gems, Strathavon, Boon St., Eckington, Nr. Pershore, Worcestershire WR10 3BL.

M. L. Beach (Products) Ltd., 41 Church St., Twickenham, Middlesex.

G. & B. Butler, 18b The Pantiles, Tunbridge Wells, Kent.

Cornerstones, 2 North Parade, Matlock Bath, Nr. Matlock, Derbyshire.

Gemset, 31 Albion St., Broadstairs, Kent.

Gemstones Ltd., 44 Walmsley St., Hull HU3 1QD.

Geobright, 28 Queens Rd., Brighton, East Sussex.

Glenjoy Lapidary Supplies, 19-21 Sun Lane, Wakefield, Yorkshire WF1 1JD.

Hirsch Jacobson Merchandising Co. Ltd., 91 Marylebone High St., London W1M 3DE.

Kernowcraft Rocks & Gems Ltd., 44 Lemon St., Truro, Cornwall.

Little Rocks, 36 Oakwood Avenue, Cardiff, Glamorgan.

Manchester Minerals, 33 School Lane, Heaton Chapel, Stockport, Greater Manchester SK4 5DE.

Manchester Minerals, 1 The Tithebarn St., off 'The Rock', Bury, Greater Manchester BL9 0JR.

Marcross Gems, 13 Market Place, Shepton Mallet, Somerset.

A. Massie & Son, 158 Burgoyne Rd., Sheffield, South Yorkshire S6 3QD.

Mineralcraft, 1 The Knoll, Crown Hill, Rayleigh, Essex SS6 7HB.

Norgems, 4 Front St., Sandbach, Cheshire.

Pebblegems, 71 St. Marks Rd., Bush Hill Park, Enfield, Middlesex EN1 1BJ.

Rockcraft, 6a Northgate, Chichester, Sussex PO19 1BA.

Rough & Tumble Ltd., 3 Tyne St., North Shields, Tyne and Wear.

Ruskins, 515 Wells Rd., Bristol, Avon.

Scotrocks, 48 Park Rd., Glasgow, Lanarkshire.

Scotrocks, 122 Rose St., South Lane, Edinburgh, Midlothian.

Scotrocks, 29 Lawn St., Paisley, Renfrewshire.

Strathclyde Studio, 'Windsor House', Harras Moor, Whitehaven, Cumbria.

The Gem Rock & Lapidary Centre, 41 Fore St., St. Just, Penzance, Cornwall.

T.L.C. World (U.K.) Ltd., 32 Craven St., London W.C.2.

Towan Lapidary Gem & Mineral Centre, 33a Bank St., Newquay, Cornwall.

Wessex Gems & Crafts, Longacre, Downs Rd., South Wonston, Winchester, Hampshire.

Whithear Lapidary Co., 35 Manor Way, North Harrow, Middlesex.